MECHANIC TRACTOR

OBJECTIVE QUESTION ANSWERS

MANOJ DOLE

Digitization is the need of the time. In the future, training in industrial training institutes will need to be conducted using online internet to make training more convenient and easy. E-books containing a set of MCQ questions will be made available to the trainees as they need to be more accustomed to the multiple choice questions MCQ to prepare for the online exams taking place in their industrial training institutes.

With all these factors in mind, Mr. Manoj Madhukar Dole Instructor, Industrial Training Institute, Satara, has written books according to the new annual system and NSQF-5 syllabus. And they've created theoretical mobile apps and blogs to make training easier, and made all these educational materials available for download on the world famous websites Google Play Store, Amazon and Apple Book Store.

The books were published by Hon'ble Joint Director Shri Rajendra Ghume Saheb Regional Office of Vocational Education and Training, Pune on 9/1/2019, at this time Shri Prakash Saigavkar Saheb Principal Government Industrial Training Institute Aundh Pune, Shri Tukaram Misal Saheb Principal Govt. Q. Sanstha Satara, Shri Sachin Dhumal Saheb District Vocational Education and Training Officer Satara, Shri Yatin Pargaonkar Saheb Principal Govt. Q. Sanstha Kolhapur, Shri Vikas Teke Saheb Inspector Vocational Education and Training Regional Office Pune, Palekar Foods Products Pvt. Ltd. Entrepreneurial Chairman of Satara Mr. Nilkanthrao Palekar Saheb, Chairman of Hira Foods Mr. Ibrahim Baba Tamboli Saheb, Mrs. Shalmali Pawar Headmaster Government Technical School Center Satara and other dignitaries were present on the occasion.

Contents

Prologue

Mechanic Tractor is a simple e-Book for ITI & Engineering Course Mechanic Tractor. It contains objective questions with underlined & bold correct answers MCQ covering all topics including all about measuring instrument and measure dimension of components and evaluate for accuracy, basic electrical, electronics and hydraulics & pneumatics, overhauling of vehicle, use proper fasteners, sheet metal operations and pipe joints, wiring circuits in vehicle and prepare different electrical joints, different weld joints, vehicle parts and accessories, Electronic diesel Control system, cooling and lubrication system, intake and exhaust systems, Tractor Transmission system, Steering, suspension, Brakes and wheel, Tyres, starting and charging system and lots more.

We add new question answers with each new version. Please email us in case of any errors/omissions. This is arguably the largest and best e-Book for All engineering multiple choice questions and answers.

As a student you can use it for your exam prep. This e-Book is also useful for professors to refresh material.

Foreword

Vocational education and training is imparted through the Department of Vocational Education and Training through the Department of Business Education and Business Practical to supply multi-skilled artisans in line with the rapidly growing demand in the industrial sector in the 21st century. All the occupations within the institutions are important, as the trainees from these occupations develop multi-skills as per the demands of the industry.

with the noble intention of making available MCQ e-books suitable for all businesses, considering that all the examinations in all the industries in the industrial sector are conducted online and include MCQ method questions. Mr. Manoj Madhukar Dole has written a very good e-book on MCQ method as per the new annual syllabus. This e-book will definitely be a guide for all the trainees, trainee candidates, training instructors and others concerned.

The author of the book is Mr. Manoj Madhukar Dole, Instructor Gov. ITI Satara has 17 years of training experience. Written as a new annual pattern, this e-book incorporates modern digital QR Code technology to understand the layout, simple language, and simple syntax, diagrams and videos for each subject. So I am sure that this e-book will definitely be useful for in-depth study and exam practice. The work they have done is certainly commendable.

Mr. Tukaram Misal
Principal Government Industrial Training Institute Satara.

Preface

DGET New Delhi and CSTARI Kolkata have been implementing an annual pattern for all businesses in ITI since the August 2018 session. The examination system will also be changed and it will be online from this year and since all the questions are of Objective Type (MCQ), the trainees are in dire need of in-depth study. It is with this in mind that we are delighted to present the books based on the old NIMI pattern and a complete overview of the new annual pattern, and we hope that these books will be a guide for all business directors and trainees. Is.

For writing these books, Johar Awate Saheb, Principal of ITI Akluj. Former Principal of ITI Satara Saigavkar Saheb, Assistant Director Shri Chandrakant Dhekne Saheb Regional Office of Vocational Education and Training, Pune, District Vocational Education and Training Officer Sachin Dhumal Saheb and Headmaster Government Technical School Kendra Shalmali Pawar Madam and son Adhiraj Dole, mother Kusum Dole, I am very grateful to my father Madhukar Dole and wife Ashwini Dole for their special guidance and cooperation from time to time.

Also, in a very short period of time, the book was reviewed by Shri Rajendra Ghume Saheb, Joint Director, Vocational Education and Training Regional Office, Pune, for his invaluable time in publishing the book. I am sincerely grateful for their feedback.

I am grateful to the Instructor of ITI Satara for there continuous support from the very beginning of writing the book.

From this book, I consider myself blessed to have shared my thoughts on e-learning with you. I will not claim that this book is perfect, because considering the perfection, this book is an attempt and is in its infancy. They will be valuable for improvement if they are tested and suggested.

Manoj Dole
Dated 9/1/2019

Acknowledgements

The industrial training and theoretical examination system of our industrial training institutes and these changes have been accepted by the craft instructors and the trainees. Theoretical examinations conducted in your industrial training institutes are also conducted online. Since these examinations are of multiple choice MCQ method, the trainees will need to get more practice of such questions.

With all these considerations in mind, Mr. Manoj Madhukar, Director, Dole Crafts, Katari Industrial Training Institute, Satara, has done a thorough study and with his diligent work and added his keen intellect, according to the new annual system and NSQF-5 syllabus, e-book of Katari and other machine trades. -Book) and they have created mobile apps and blogs on theoretical topics to make training easier and have made all these educational materials available for download on the world famous websites Google Play Store, Amazon and Apple Book Store. Training has been made easier by creating a print version and using advanced techniques like QR Code.

All these educational materials will definitely be a guide for all the trainees for in-depth study and for the craft instructors and other concerned who are imparting vocational training.

Mechanic Tractor MCQ Drawings

Online Test Exam
ITI Books
CNC Course
AutoCAD CAM
JOB & Apprentice
Online Theory
Computer Course
Trading Course
Web Designing
MSCIT Course
Shopping Business
Internet Business
Remotasks Course
Online Services
Top Sportsmans
Indian Army
Freedom Fighters
Top Scientists
Social Reformers
Motivational Speaker
Top Richest People
Join WhatsApp Group
Join Facebook Group
Like Facebook Page
PAN / Adhar / Licence
Passport

Fire extinguisher

Calliper

Hacksaw frame

Universal surface guage

Hammer

Centre punch

Bench vice

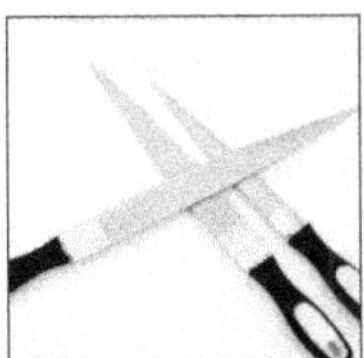

Files

Scraper

Surface Plate

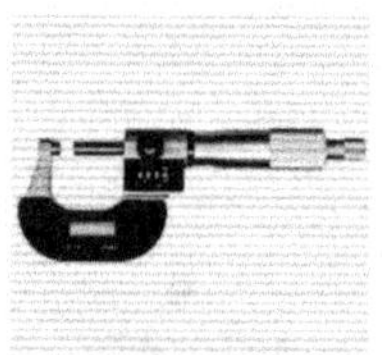 

Outside Micrometer

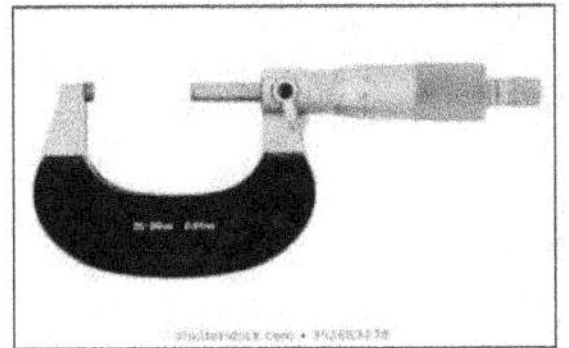 

Micrometer

Depth micrometer

Vernier Calliper

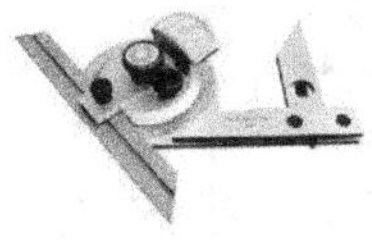 

Vernier bevel protractor

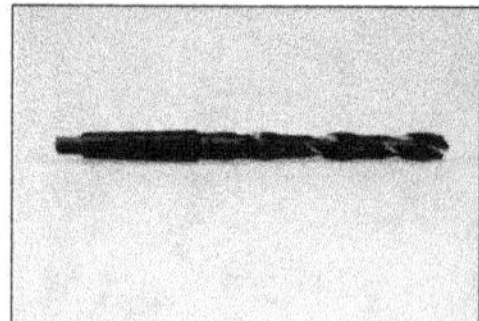

Drilling

Reamer

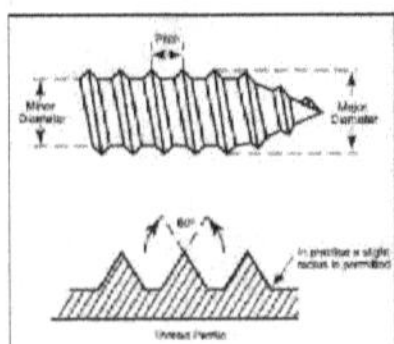

Thread

Tap Die

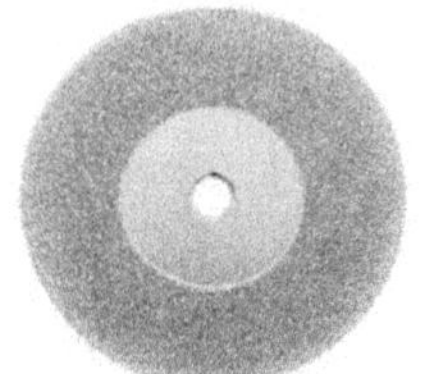 

Grinding Wheel

Slip gauge

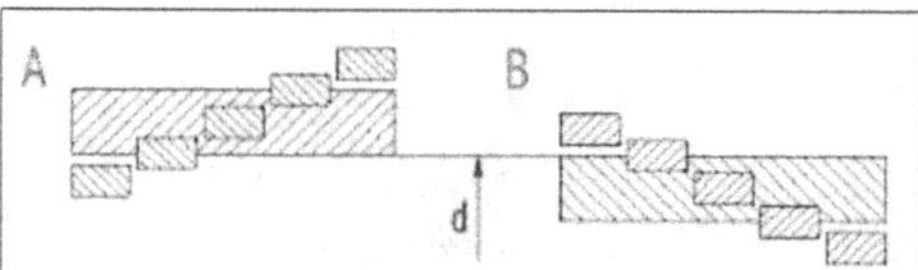 

Limit fit tolerance

taper ring gauge

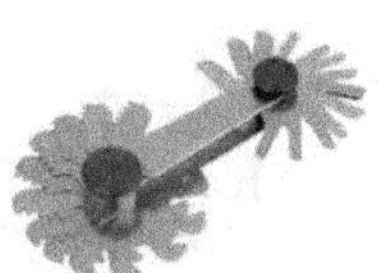 

screw pitch gauge

Gear

screw pitch gauge

Tap Die

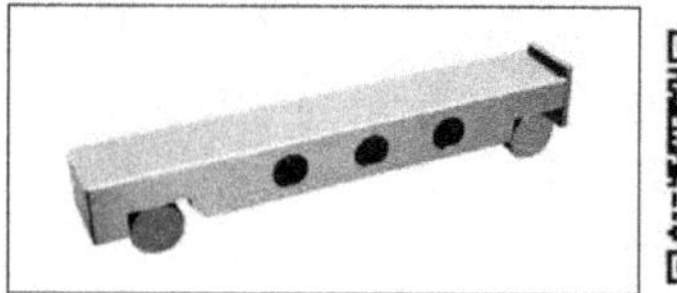

Sine bar

Slip gauge

Dial test indicator

Telescopic gauge

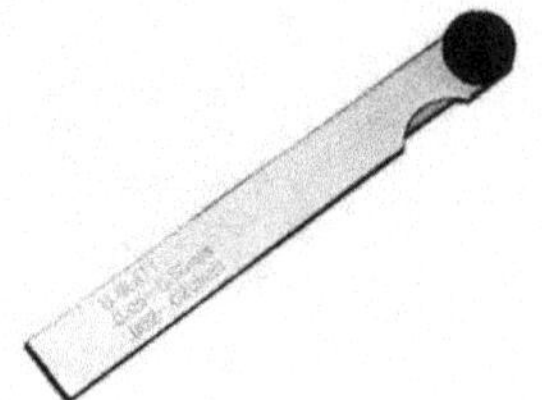

Feeler gauge

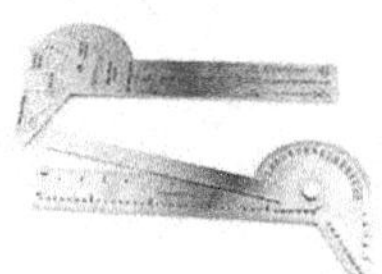

Centre gauge

Jig

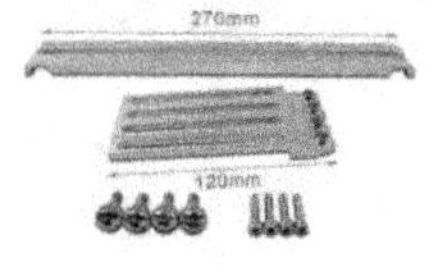

Fixture

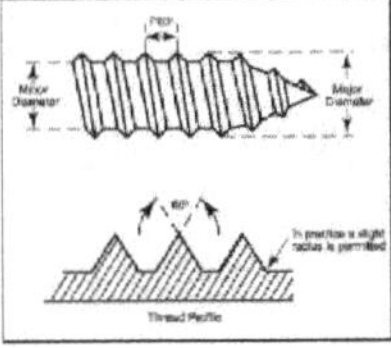

Thread

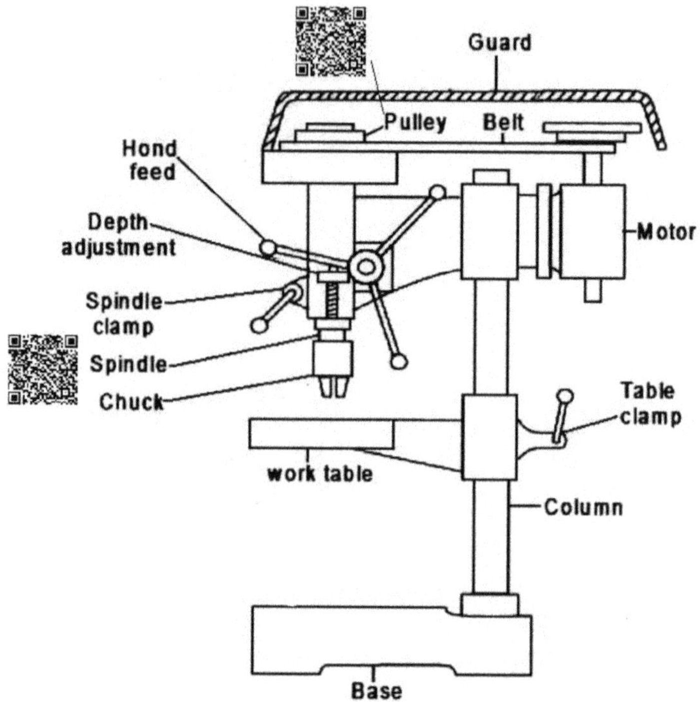

Piller Drilling Machine

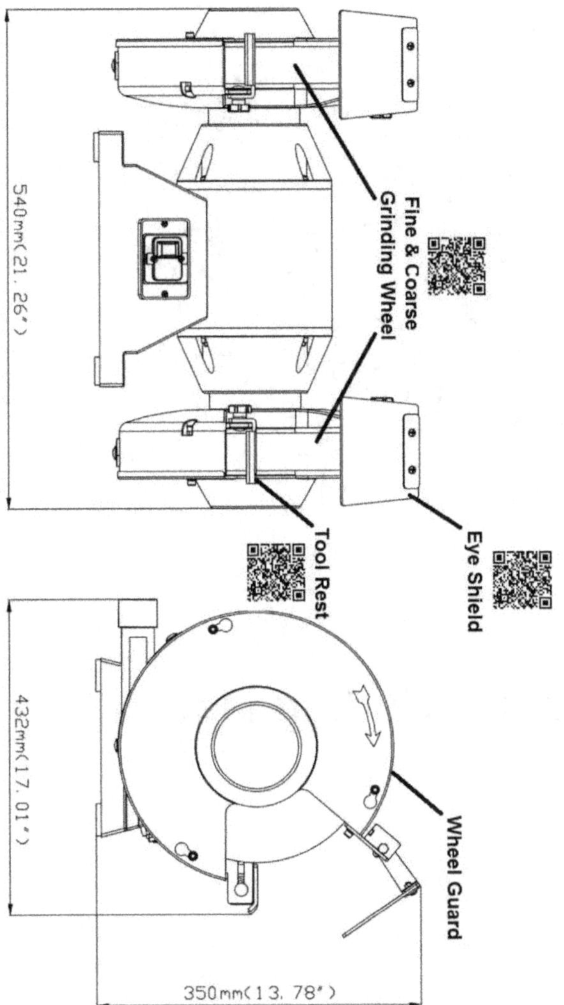

Bench Grinding Machine
540mm(21. 26")
Fine & Coarse
Grinding Wheel
Eye Shield
Tool Rest
432mm(17. 01")
350mm(13. 78")
Wheel Guard

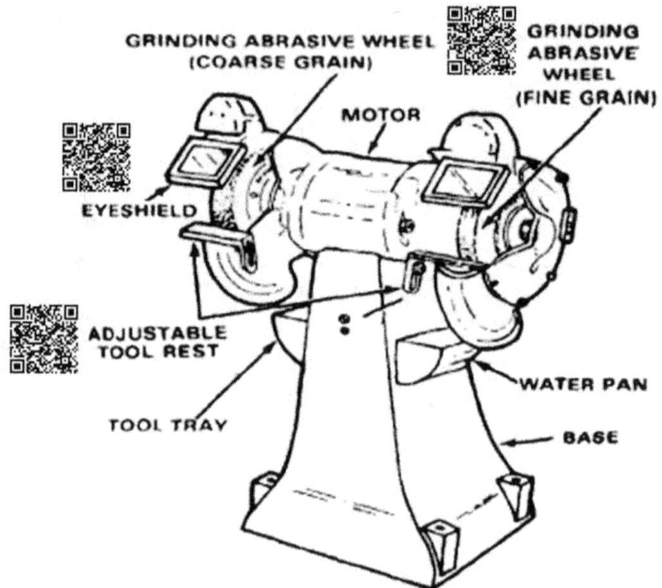

Pedastal Grinding Machine

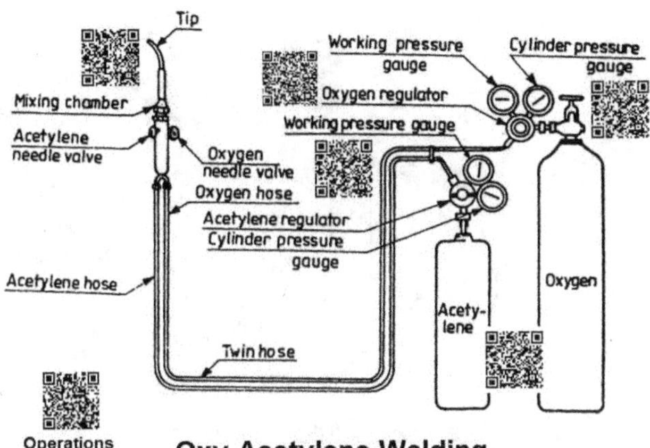

Oxy Acetylene Welding

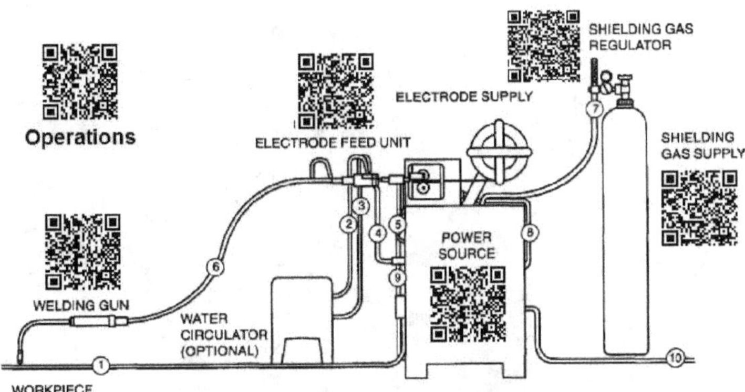

Gas Metal Arc Welding

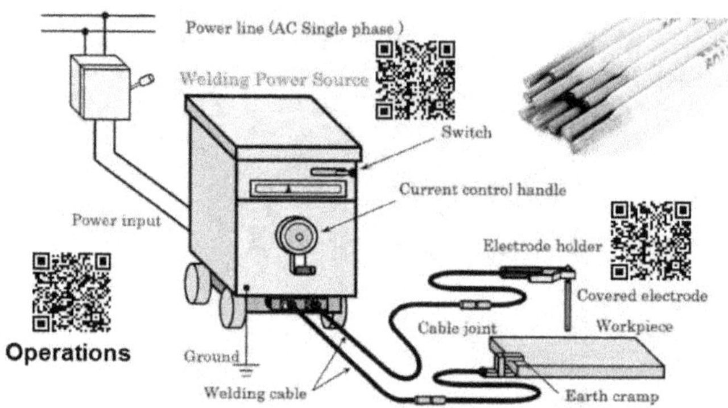

Shielded Metal Arc Welding

Auto Coolant System

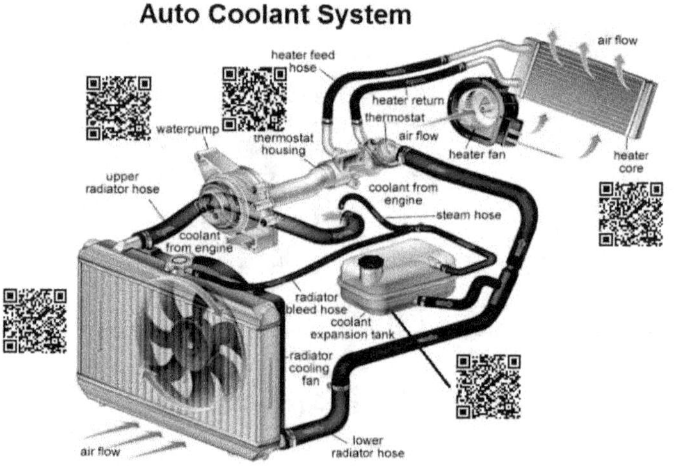

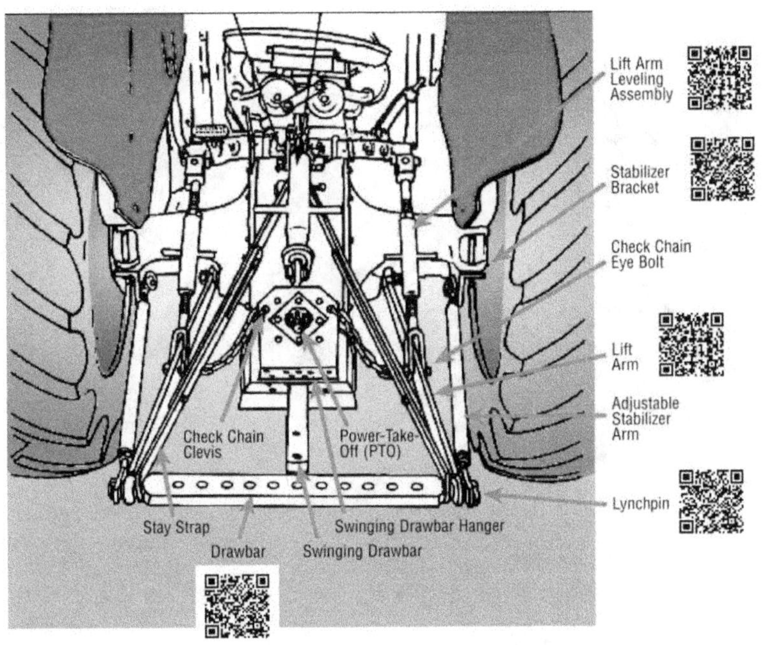

Lift Arm Leveling Assembly
Stabilizer Bracket
Check Chain Eye Bolt
Lift Arm
Adjustable Stabilizer Arm
Lynchpin
Check Chain Clevis
Power-Take-Off (PTO)
Stay Strap
Swinging Drawbar Hanger
Drawbar
Swinging Drawbar

Tractor Case Parts

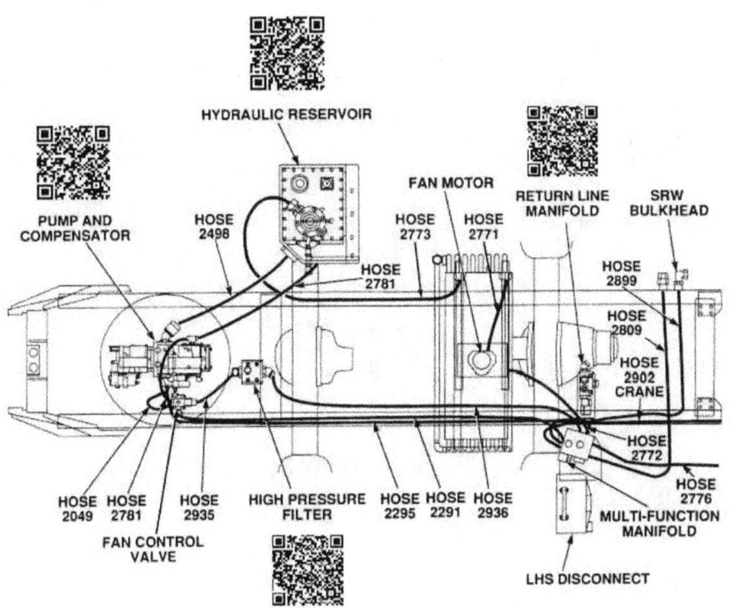

Tractor Hydraulic System

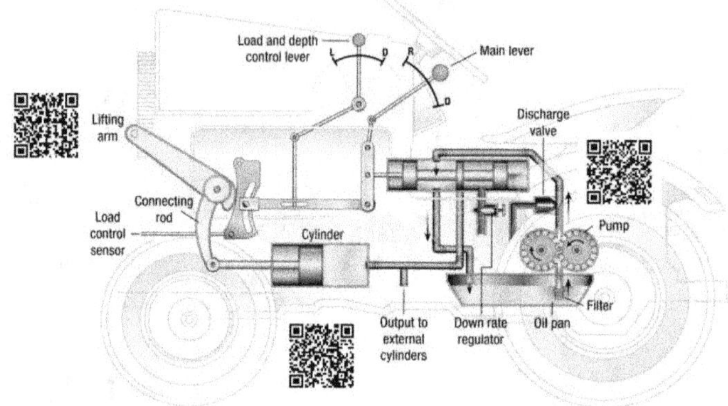

Tractor Hydraulic Elevetor

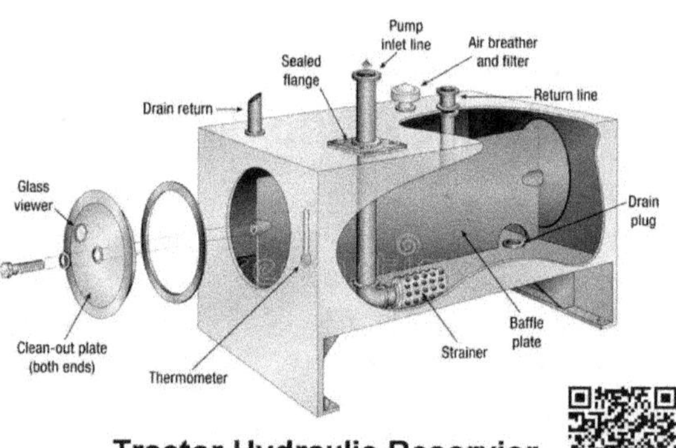

Tractor Hydraulic Resorvior

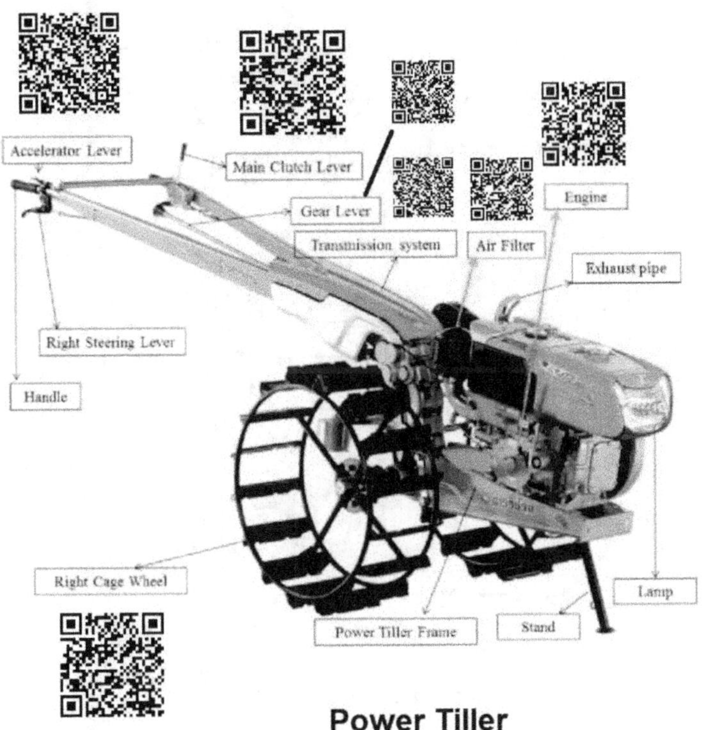

Power Tiller

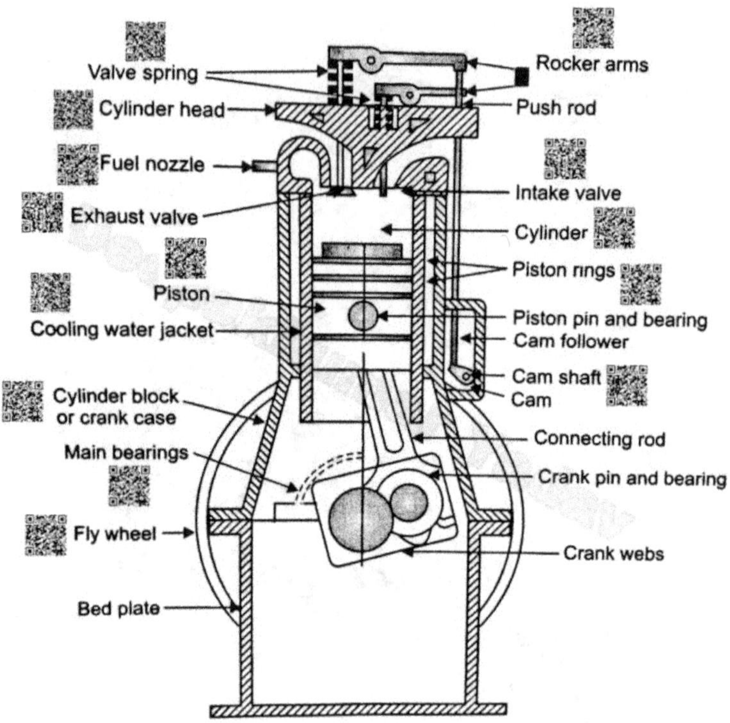

Components of Diesel Engine

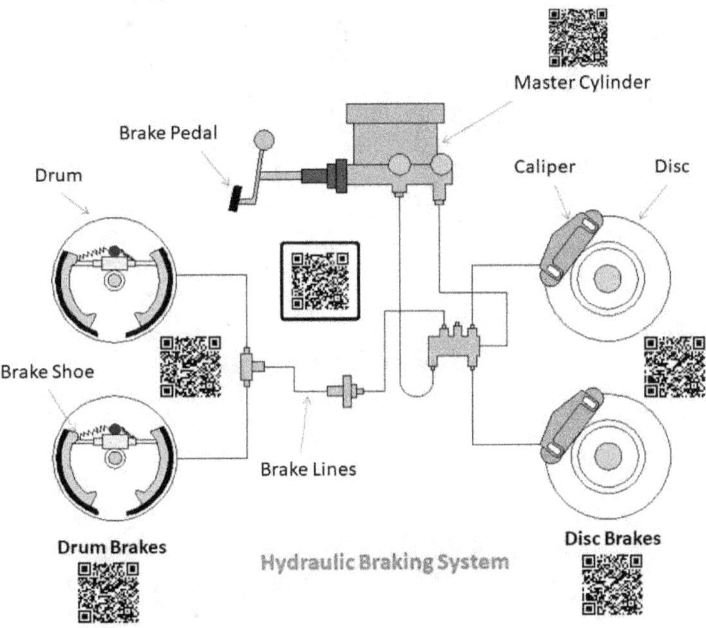
Master Cylinder
Brake Pedal
Drum
Caliper
Disc
Brake Shoe
Brake Lines
Drum Brakes
Disc Brakes
Hydraulic Braking System

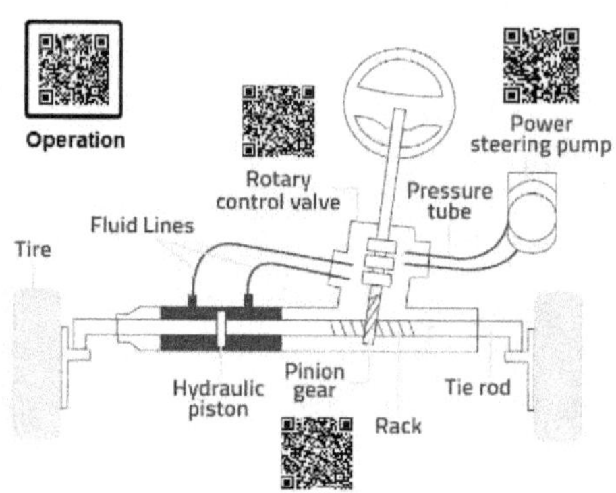

Power Steering System

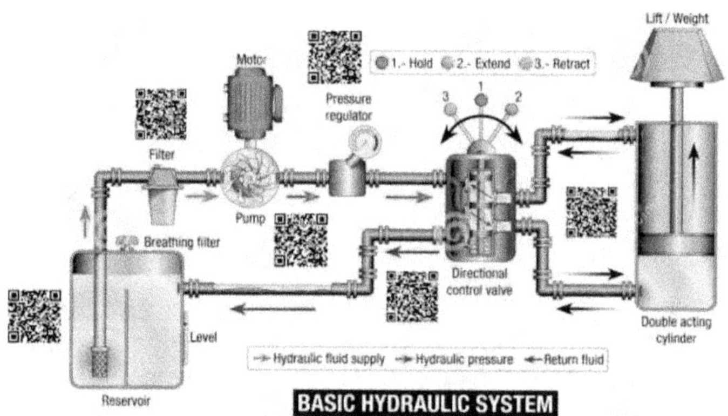

CHAPTER TWO

Mechanic Tractor

1] Which one is a workshop safety?

A] Keep shop floor clean and free from grease, oil or other slippery materials

B] Stop the machine before changing the speed

C] Don't use cracked or chipped tools

D] Don't try to stop a running machine with hand

2] In Personal Protect Equipment (PPE] HELMET is used to

A] protect head

B] Protect eyes

C] Protect hands

D] Protect ears

3] Which of the following belongs to general safety?

A Have a worker in good attitude

B] The work clean and clear

C] Concentrate on your work

D] Keep the floor and gangways clean and clear

4] While grinding, which is used to protect the eyes?

A] Dark green glass

B] Mask

C] Sun glasses

D] Safety goggles

5] Which of the following is done for machine safety?

A] Check the oil level before starting the machine

B] Do things in a methodical way

C] Keep the floor and gangways clean and clear

D] Don't use dies and scarves

6] In Personal Protect Equipment (PPE], 'sleeves' is used to protect

----

A] Face
B] Eyes
C] Ears
<u>D] Hands</u>
7] ABC stands for --------------
A] Automatic Breathing Control
B] Automatic Blood Control
<u>C] Airway Breathing Circulation</u>
D] Automatic Blood Circulation
8] Fire & FIRE EXTINGUISHERS

fire extingusher

Fire Extingusher

Fire extinguisher

9] To put off"Class B" fire, the types of fire extinguisher used is ....
<u>A] dry power</u>
B] Carbon dioxide
C] Jet of water
D] Foam type
10] Which type of fire extinguisher is used to put off general fire?
<u>A] Water type Extinguisher</u>
B] Foam type Extinguisher
C] Dry chemical powder Extinguisher
D] Carbon dioxide (C02] Extinguisher
11] In case of bleeding, take treatment Of
D] cold 3" and rest
<u>A] spray cold water</u>
B] Bandage immediately -----.
B] Enquire about the accident thought treatment

safety   workshop safety

12] in case of an accident, the victim should im

A] Asked to take rest

C] Attended immediately

D] leave him

13] First aid is given to an injured or ill person primarily....

A] Save life

B] Prevent further deterioration of the muff's

C] Give best possible comfort

D] All of these

14] Colour code for Bins for waste paper segregation is -----

A] blue Colour

B] Yellow Colour

C] Red Colour

D] Green Colour

15] In Japanese Seiko stands for --------------

A] Shine

B] Sort

C] Standardize

D] Sustain

16] Benefit of SS system is ------

A] Increase in productivity

B] Increase in quality

C] Reduction in wastage of time

D] All of these

17] Safety is -----------

A] nobody's business

B] every bodise business

C] Some bodies business

D] The organization business

18] For basic categories of safety signs are available The meaning of"prohibition" sign ----

A] shows it must not be done
B] Shows what must be done
C] Warns the hazard or danger
D] Gives information of safety provision
18] One micrometer (U] is equal to...
A] 0.1mm
B] 0.01mm
C] 0.001mm
D] 0.0001mm
19] The caliper meant for measuring the width of a slot is...
A] Odd leg caliper
B] Outside caliper
C] Jenny caliper
D] Inside calliper

caliper   hand tools

Calliper
20] The size of the dividers are specified by the -----------
A] Total length of legs
B] Distance between the points when fully opened
C] Length of legs without points
D] distance between the pivot and the point
21] The instrument used to mark parallel lines, parallel to the datum edge is -
A] jenny caliper
B] Divider
C] Outside calliper
D] Inside calliper
22] Which one of the following is an indirect measuring tool?
A] Outside caliper
B] Vernier calliper
C] Steel rule

D] Outside micrometer

23] For cutting thin tubing, the most suitable pitch of the hacksaw blade is...

A] 1.8mm

B] 1.4mm

C] 1mm

D] <u>0.8mm</u>

24] For cutting solid brass, the most suitable pitch of the hacksaw blade is...

A] <u>1.8mm</u>

B] 1.4mm

C] 1mm

D] 0.8mm

hacksaw   Hacksaw Frame Blade

Hacksaw frame

25] A new hacksaw blade after a few strokes becomes loose because of the...

A] <u>Stretching of the blade</u>

B] Wing-nut threads being worn out

C] Wrong pitch of the blade

D] Improper selection of the set of saws.

26] While cutting small diameter pipes, it is advisable to watch regularly and ensure that...

A] The cut is along the curved line

B] <u>More saw teeth are in contract</u>

C] The work is not overheated

D] Proper balancing of hacksaw is maintained

27] The vice clamps are used to...

A] Protect hard jaws

B] Clamp the work pieces rigidly

C] <u>Protect the finished surfaces</u>

D] Prevent the movable jaw being filed

28] The reference surface during marking is provided by the...

A] Surface gauge

B] Workpiece

C] Drawing of the work

D] <u>Marking table surface</u>

29] The size of an engineer's vice is specified by the...

A] Length of the movable jaw

B] <u>Width of the jaws</u>

C] Height of the vice

D] Maximum opening of the jaws

30] The part of the universal surface gauge which helps to draw a parallel line along a datum edge is the..

A] Rocker arm

B] Snug

C] Fine adjustment screw

D] <u>Guide pins</u>

universal surface
gauge   Surface Gauge

Universal surface guage

31] Scribers are made of...

A] Mild steel

B] <u>High carbon steel</u>

C] Brass

D] Cast iron

32] Portion of the hammer used for fixing the handle is...

A] Face

B] Peen

C] Cheek

D] <u>Eye hole</u>

33] Weight of the hammer for the marking purpose is...

A] <u>250g</u>

B] 500g

C] 1 kg

D] 2 kgs

hammer   Hammers

Hammer

34] The size of the dividers are specified by the...

A] Total length of the legs

B] Distance between the points when fully opened

C] Length of legs without the points

D] <u>Distance between the pivot and the point</u>

35] The included angle of the groove of 'V' block is always....

A] 45°

B] 60°

C] 90°

D] <u>120°</u>

36] 'V' blocks are available in grades of...

A] <u>A & B</u>

B] A,B & C

C] 1,2 & 3

D] 1 & 2

37] 'V' blocks of grade 'B' are made of

A] <u>Cast iron</u>

B] Mild steel

C] Steel

D] Cast steel

38] Name the punch used to locate the centre.

A] Prick punch 30°

B] Prick punch 60°

C] Centre punch

D] Dot punch

Centre punch 1   Punches

Centre punch

39] The point angle of centre punch is --------

A] 30°

B] 50°

c] 900

D] 1200

40] Punches are used for forming ---------of any shape

A] Holes

B] Mining

C] Knurling

D] Reaming

41] Generally the length of the handle of the vice is ----------

A] 1.5 times the normal size of the vice

B] 2.5 times the normal size of the vice

C] 3.5 times the normal size of the vice

D] 4.5 times the normal size of the vice

bench vice　　　　　　　　　　Bench Vice

Bench vice

42] Bench vice spindle is made of ....

A] mild steel

B] Cast iron

C] Tool steel

D] Bronze

43] The convexity of files helps...

A] To file concave surfaces

B] To file convex surfaces

C] To prevent rounding of edges of work

D] The file to become straight when pressure is applied

files 1　　　　　　　　　　Files

Files

44] Which file used for filling wood, leather and other soft material? .

A] Single cut file

B] Double cut file

c] Rasp cut file

D] Curved cut file

45] File used is used for ------------

A] Cleaning the work piece

C] Renewing the file teeth

B] cleaning the file teeth

D] Cleaning the chips

46] File card is used to --------

A] Clean the work piece

C] Renew the file teeth

B] Clean the file teeth

47] The point angle of scriber is -----------

A] 30°

B] 60°

C] 5° to 10°

D] 12° to 15°

48] The cutting angle for chipping cast iron is...

A] 37.5°

B] 55°

C] 60°

D] 90°

chisel   hand tools

49] The chisel will dig into the material when...

A] The rake angle is more

B] The clearance angle is too low

C] The angle of inclination is more

D] The angle of inclination is too low

50] A slight convexity is given to the cutting edge to...

A] Cut curved surfaces

B] Cut sharp corners

C] Prevent digging of the ends

D] Allow the lubricant to enter

51] Surface plates are made of...

A] High grade cast steel

B] Fine-grained cast iron

C] Alloy steels

D] Wrought iron

Surface plates   hand tools

52] Surface plates are specified by their length and breadth & are in

A] decimetre

B] Cubic meter

C] Cylindrical

53] Ribs are given on the unmachined portion of the angle plate for...

A] Easy handling

B] Convenience in manufacturing

C] Clamping while setting on machines

D] Rigidity and to prevent distortion

54] The slots on the angle plate are given for...

A] Reducing weight

B] Aligning the work

C] Lifting using hooks

D] Accommodating bolts.

55] The size of the angle plates is stated by...

A] Weight

B] Length

C] Length x width

D] Size number

56] for high speed parting off work on material like cemented carbide Is'

A] Do all machine

B] Cutting off machine

C] Heavy duty power saw

D] Mining machine sitting saw

57] Gun metal is an alloy of copper, ------------

A] tin and zinc

B] Lead and zinc

C] Zinc and nickel

D] Lead and nickel

58] Cast iron is used for manufacturing machine beds because -------

A] it can resist more compressive stress

B] it is heavy in weight

C] It is cheaper metal

D] It is a brittle metal

59] Accuracy or least count of a metric outside micrometric is ---------

A] 0-1 mm

B] <u>0.01 mm</u>

C] 0.001 mm

D] 0.02 mm

micrometer   Out Side Micrometer

60] 1000 microns means -----

A] <u>1 mm</u>

B] 1 m

C] 1000 mm

D] 10 cm

61] in a metric micrometer, a complete revolution of thimble advances
----

A] 0.01 mm

B] 0.25 mm

C] <u>0.50 mm</u>

D] 1.00mm

micrometer2   Out Side Micrometer

Micrometer

62] Ratchet Stop in the micrometer helps to ------------

A] <u>Control the pressure</u>

B] lock the spindle

C] Adjust the zero error

D] Hold the work piece

63] 1000 micron means ------------

A] 1 mm

B] 1 m

C] 1000 mm

D] 10 cm

64] What is the zero reading of a 50-75 mm outside micrometer?

A] 0.000 mm

B] 0.01 mm

C] 25.00 mm

D] 50.00 mm

65] The value of the smallest division on sleeve of a metric outside micrometer is -----

A] 0.50 mm

B] 1.00 mm

C] 1.50 mm

D] 2.00 mm

66] Ratchet stop in the micrometer helps to ---------

A] control the pressure

B] Lock the spindle

C] Adjust the zero error

D] Hold the work piece

67] Least count of depth micrometer is

A] 0.5 mm

B] 0.2 mm

C] 0.001 mm

D] 0.01 mm

Depth micrometer 1   Depth Micrometer

Depth micrometer

68] The least count of vernier calliper is (main scale = 49 division, vernier scale = 50 division]

A] 0.1 mm

B] 0.01 mm

C] 0.001 mm

D] 0.02 mm

vernier calliper 1   Vernier Caliper 1

Vernier Calliper

69] The type of measurement made by using a Vernier Calliper is -------

A] Direct measurement

B] Indirect measurement

C] 90"] (a] 81 (b]

D] None of these

70] The least count of a vernier bevel protractor is...

A] 1"

B] 5'

C] 1°

D] 5°

71] The part of a vernier bevel protractor which is normally used as a reference base for measuring angles is the...

A] Blade

B] <u>Stock</u>

C] Disc

C] Main scale

vernier bevel protractor   Vernier Bevel

3   Protractor

Vernier bevel protractor

72] The part of a vernier bevel protector on which main scale divisions are marked is the...

A] Stock

B] Dial

C] <u>Disc</u>

D] Adjustable blade

73] The part of a bevel protractor, which comes in contact with the inclined surface while measuring is the...

A] <u>Blade</u>

B] Stock

C] Disc

D] Dial

74] The value of each division of the main scale of a vernier bevel protractor is...

A] 5'

B] <u>1°</u>

C] 5°

D]10°

75] The value of each division of the vernier scale of a bevel protractor is...

A] 1°

B] 1∘5'

C] 1∘55'

D] 5'

76] The taper shank drills are held on the machine by means of...

A] Chucks

B] Sleeves

C] Drift

D] Vice

taper shank drills   drilling machine

77] Drill chucks are fitted on the drilling machine spindle by means of a...

A] Knurled ring

B] Arbor

C] Drift

D] Pinion and key

78] The Morse taper provided on drills ranges between...

A] MT 1 to MT 5

B] MT 1 to MT 4

C] MT 0 to MT 5

D] MT 0 to MT 4

79] A drift is used for...

A] Drawing a drill location

B] Fixing chuck on the machine spindle

C] Removing a broken drill from the work

D] Removing the drill from the machine spindle

80] When the taper shank of the drill is larger than the machine spindle, the device to hold the drill is a...

A] Drill sleeve

B] Taper socket

C] Drill drift

D] Chuck and key

81] The suitable cutting fluid for drilling mild steel in a drilling machine is...

A] Synthetic soluble oil

B] Neat oil

C] Distilled water

D] <u>Soluble oil</u>

82] A special feature of the radial drilling machine is...

A] It can be used for drilling with a H.S.S. drill

B] Table can be moved and set at any position

C] A variety of speeds is available

D] <u>The spindle can be brought to any position</u>

piller drilling machine   drilling-machine-spindle

83] The point angle of drills depends on...

A] The size of the drill

B] The type of machine

C] <u>The material of the work</u>

D] The RPM of the drill

84] The point angle for a standard drill is...

A] 60°

B] 108°

C] <u>118°</u>

D] 135°

85] The helical angle determines the...

A] Cutting angle

B] Chew angle

C] <u>Rake angle</u>

D] Lip angle

86] The clearance angle of the drill is between...

A] 3° to 5°

B] <u>8° to 12°</u>

C] 12° to 20°
D] 15° to 20°
87] In a remote place (no electricity available] a rail track is to be drilled. Choose the right drilling machine
A] Radial drilling machine
B] Pillar drilling machine
C] <u>Ratchet drilling machine</u>
D] Sensitive drilling Machine
       drilling   drilling machine

Drilling
88] A drilling machine used by a carpenter for cabinet making is a...
A] Ratchet drilling machine
B] Radial drilling machine
C] <u>Breast drilling machine</u>
D] Sensitive drilling machine
89] Which one of the following drilling machines is used for drilling holes where electricity is not available?
A] Bench drilling machine
B] Pillar drilling machine
C] Redial drilling machine
D] <u>Ratchet drilling machine</u>
90] Which one of the following drilling machine is used for heavy duty work?
A] Bench drilling machine
B] Pillar drilling machine
C] <u>Radial drilling machine</u>
D] Electric hand drilling machine
91] Drill chuck are held on the machine spindle by means of ------
A] <u>arbor</u>
B] Drift
C] draw-in bar

D] Chuck nut

92] Different speeds are obtained in a sensitive bench drilling machine by ----

<u>A] Belt pulley mechanism</u>

B] Hydraulic mechanism

C] Rack and Pinion mechanism

D] Cam and follower mechanism

93] The process of heating and cooling to change the structure of steel for obtaining the required properties is called

A] Hardening

<u>B] Normalizing</u>

C] Heat treatment

D] Tempering

94] The main purpose of annealing is to

A] Increase the hardness

B] Increase the toughness

<u>C] Improve machinability</u>

D] Improve distortion

95] The purpose of normalizing steel is to -----------

<u>A] Remove the induced Stress</u>

B] Improve genes and reduce brittleness

C] Soften the metal

D] Increase the surface?

96] Which one of the following process is used for hardenmg the outer 5" Annealing

A] Hardening

B] Tempering

<u>C] Case Hardening</u>

D] Tear surface

97] The purpose of producmg a component with tough and ductIle core and hard ou is known as......

A] Hardening

<u>B] Case hardening</u>

C] Tempering

D] annealing

98] Lower critical temperature of high carbon steel while hardening is -----------

A] 9600C

B] 900°C

c] 7230 c

D] 56O C

99] The process of Changing the structure and thus changing the properties by heating and 'cooling is known as

A] Heat treatment

B] Alloying

C] Tempering

D] None of these

100] For refining the grain structure which one of the following heat treatment processes 'Is adopted.

A] Annealing

B] Hardening

C] Tempering

D] Normalising

101] Annealing is performed on iron and steel ---------

A] To remove internal stresses

B] To reduce hardness

C] To improve machinability

D] All of these

102] Which one of the following does not fall under the stages of heat treatment?

A] Heating

B] Cleaning

C] Quenching

D] Soaking

20] METAL 02

103] Gun metal is an alloy of copper, ------------

A] tin and zinc

B] Lead and zinc

C] Zinc and nickel

D] Lead and nickel

104] for making gutters, roof flashing, hoods etc.

A] Galvanised iron

B] Stainless steel

C] Copper sheet

D] Metal sheets

105] in dairies. food processing, kitchen ware etc.

A] Galvanised iron
B] <u>Stainless steel</u>
C] Copper sheet
D] Metal sheets
106] for making buckets, heating ducts, cabinets etc.
A] <u>Galvanised iron</u>
B] Stainless steel
C] Copper sheet
D] Metal sheets
107] Punching a number of holes in a sheet is known as?
a) <u>Perforating</u>
b) Parting
c) Notching
d) Lancing
108] Shearing the sheet into two or more pieces is known as?
a) Perforating
b) <u>Parting</u>
c) Notching
d) Lancing
109] Removing the pieces from the edge in shearing operation is known as?
a) Perforating
b) Parting
c) <u>Notching</u>
d) Lancing
110] Leaving a tab without removing any material is known as?
a) Perforating
b) Parting
c) Notching
d) <u>Lancing</u>
111] Moving a small straight punch up and down rapidly into a die is done by a process known as?
a) Perforating
b) Parting
c) <u>Nibbling</u>
d) Lancing
112] As the thickness of sheet is increased the clearance needed will also?

a) <u>Increase</u>
b) Decrease
c) No effect
d) First decrease then increase
113] Bevelling is particularly suitable for shearing of?
a) Thin blanks
b) <u>Thick blanks</u>
c) Very thin blanks
d) None of the Mentioned
114] Which of the following is a type of die?
a) Simple dies
b) Progressive dies
c) Compound die
d) <u>All of the Mentioned</u>
115] Which of the following die can perform multiple operations such as blanking, punching, notching etc.?
a) Simple dies
b) <u>Progressive dies</u>
c) Compound die
d) None of the Mentioned
116] As the clearance increases, the punch force required?
a) <u>Decreases</u>
b) Increases
c) Remains same
d) First increases then decrease
117] Maximum temperature for forging H. S. S. is -------------degree.
A] 1200
B] 100
C] <u>1100</u>
D] 1500
118] Main purpose Of annealing is -----------.
A] <u>to improve machinability</u>
B] to improve magnetism
C] to increase hardness
D] to increase toughness
119] The carbon percentage in H.S.S. tool is -------
A] <u>0.75 to 1.00 %</u>
B] 1.00 to 2.00 00

C] 0.60 to 0.75 %

D] 0.02 to 0.03 %.

120] Which one of the following is the resistance of a metal to elastic deformation?

A] Ductility.

B] Strength

C] Stiffness

D] Toughness

121] in canneries and chemical plants Metal sheets

A] Galvanised iron

B] Stainless steel

C] Copper sheet

D] Metal sheets

122] Alloy steel, good corrosive resistance and welds easily

A] Black iron

B] Galvanised iron

C] Stainless steel

D] Aluminium

123] Cheapest, can be rolled to any desired thickness

A] Black iron

B] Galvanised iron

C] Stainless steel

D] Aluminium

124] Resists against rust bright silvery appearance

A] Black iron

B] Galvanised iron

C] Stainless steel

D] Aluminium

125] Corrodes rapidly. Bluish black appearance

A] Black iron

B] Galvanised iron

C] Stainless steel

D] Aluminium

126] Drill a blind hole equal to half of the diameter of the stud. Insert this tool into the hole and remove the stud by turning this anticlockwise.

A] Prick Punch Method

B] Filing square very mm

C] Using square taper punch

D] Ezy-out method

127] If the stud is broken near to the surface, employ this method to remove the stud.

A] <u>Prick Punch Method</u>

B] Filing square very mm

C] Using square taper punch

D] Ezy-out method

128] When a stud is broken a little above the surface this method is used to remove the stud.

A] Filing square very mm

B] Using square taper punch

C] Ezy-out method

D] <u>Making drill hole</u>

129] To extract the broken stud a special tool is employed in this method.

A] Prick Punch Method

B] Filing square very mm

C] Using square taper punch

D] <u>Ezy-out method</u>

130] File the protruding stud into square form and remove it.

A] Prick Punch Method

B] <u>Filing square very mm</u>

C] Using square taper punch

D] Ezy-out method

131] Ammonium chloride is used as a flux for soldering...

A] <u>steel</u>

B] aluminium

C] galvanized iron

D] stainless steel

132] Soldering of M.S sheets takes place at a temperature of...

A] 150°C

B] <u>250°C</u>

C] 400°C

D] 850°C

133.] In soldering operation the base metal is...

A.] <u>not heated</u>

B.] heated to 200°C

C.] heated to 650◦C

D.] heated to red hot condition

134] Rivets for Joining sheets to thick plates.

A] <u>Countersunk head</u>

B] Flat head

C] Pan head

D] Mushroom

135] Rivets for Joining sheet metal.

A] Countersunk head

B] <u>Flat head</u>

C] Pan head

D] Mushroom

136] Rivets for Heavy fabrication work.

A] Countersunk head

B] Flat head

C] <u>Pan head</u>

D] Mushroom

137] Rivets for Reduces the height of rivet head above the meta\ surface

A] Countersunk head

B] Flat head

C] Pan head

D] <u>Mushroom</u>

138] Rivets for commonly used for structural work.

A] Countersunk head

B] Flat head

C] Pan head

D] <u>Snap head</u>

139] The pressure of acetylene gas for gas cutting a 10mm M.S plate is...

A.] <u>0.15 kgf/cm2</u>

B.] 0.5 kgf/cm2

C.] 1.0 kgf/cm2

D.] 1.5 kgf/cm2

140] What size of the cutting nozzle you will select for cutting 10mm thick mild steel?

A.] 0.8 mm

B.] <u>1.2 mm</u>

C.] 1.6 mm

D.] 2.0 mm

141] The angle of filler rod in case of rightward welding technique is...

A.] 10 to 20°

B.] 20 to 30°

C.] <u>30 to 40°</u>

D.] 40 to 50°

142] One of the advantages of the high pressure system of gas welding is...

A.] it is cheaper

B.] <u>it is portable</u>

C.] it is less dangerous

D.] it does not require a skilled welder

143] The function of a gas regulator is...

A.] get different types of flames

B.] mix the gases in the required proportion

C.] change the volume of gas flowing to the blow pipe

D.] <u>set the working pressure</u>

gas welding

Oxy Acetylene Welding

144] For welding a lap fillet joint in vertical position by gas what should be the angle of below pipe to the line of weld?

A.] 30° to 40°

B.] 45°to 50°

C.] 60° to 70°

D.] 75° to 80°

145] Which metal pipe should NOT be used for passing acetylene gas in order to avoid explosions?

A.] galvanized iron

B.] stainless steel

C.] mild steel

D.] cooper

146] he percentage of carbon in acetylene gas is...

A.] 99%

B.] 92.3%

C.] 89.1%

D.] 85.3%

147] Acetylene gas contains

A.] calcium, carbon and hydrogen

B.] calcium and hydrogen

C.] calcium, carbon, hydrogen and oxygen

D.] carbon and hydrogen

148] In an acetylene purifier the sulphureted and phosphorated hydrogen are removed by...

A.] pumice

B.] water

C.] filter wool

D.] purifying chemicals

149] One of the functions of flux in gas welding is...

A.] dissolve the metal oxides

B.] reduce the melting point of mental

C.] increase the flame temperature

D.] increase the root penetration

150] On which of the following factors, the choice of flux for gas welding depend?

A.] type of material to be joined

B.] type of edge penetration

C.] type of fuel gas

D.] type of flame used

151] The divergence allowance required for gas welding a 300mm long copper butt joint is...

A.] 1 to 2 mm

B.] 2 to 3 mm

C.] <u>3 to 4 mm</u>

D.] 4 to 5 mm

152] The type of edge preparation done for gas welding a 4mm thick copper butt joint is...

A.] single bevel

B.] <u>single V</u>

C.] double V

D.] square

153] The size of nozzle used to gas weld 3.15 mm thick aluminium butt joint is...

A.] 13

B.] 10

C.] 7

D.] <u>5</u>

154] What is the value of preheating temperature for gas welding of aluminium?

A.] 100 to 120∘C

B.] <u>150 to 180∘C</u>

C.] 180 to 200∘C

D.] 210 to 250∘C

155] Name the tool used to make and finish the leak proof joints of a pipe T joint

A.] <u>groover</u>

B.] setting hammer

C.] creasing hammer

D.] round bottom stake

156] The angle of vee groove of a single vee but joint for cast iron welding is...

A.] 60∘

B.] 70∘

C.] 80∘

D.] <u>90∘</u>

157] Shielded metal arc welding is classified under the process of...

A.] electric resistance welding

B.] special welding

C.] electric arc welding

D.] electro gas welding

158] How to specify the size of an electrode holder?

A.] by its weight

B.] by its shape

C.] by its current carrying capacity

D.] by the metal used for making it

159] The current set for a 3.15mm medium coated mild steel electrode is...

A.] 50 to 80 amp

B.] 90 to 120 amp

C.] 120 to 150 amp

D.] 150 to 170 amp

160] A long arc is used in...

A.] welding with a low hydrogen electrode

B.] horizontal position

C.] plug or slot welding

D.] cast iron welding

161] If the travel speed of electrode is high, which type of weld defect you will get on a T fillet joint?

A.] overlap

B.] slag inclusion

C.] excessive reinforcement

D.] lack of root penetration

162] Which weld defect occurs on a lap fillet joint due to improper weaving of the electrode in the covering/final run?

A.] crack

B.] undercut

C.] lack of fusion

D.] edge of plate melted off

163] Which one of the following is used in the oxy-arc cutting process?

A.] flux coated solid electrode

B.] bare wire tubular electrode

C.] flux coated tubular electrode

D.] bare tungsten arc cutting electrode

164] The electrode holder in a carbon arc cutting equipment is made up of...

A.] plain carbon steel

B.] galvanized iron

C.] <u>aluminium</u>

D.] copper

165] The taper shank drills are held on the machine by means of...

A. Chucks

<u>B. Sleeves</u>

C. Drift

D. Vice

166] Drill chucks are fitted on the drilling machine spindle by means of a...

A.] Knurled ring

<u>B.] Arbor</u>

C.] Drift

D.] Pinion and key

167] The Morse taper provided on drills ranges between...

A.] <u>MT 1 to MT 5</u>

B.] MT 1 to MT 4

C.] MT 0 to MT 5

D.] MT 0 to MT 4

168] A drift is used for...

A.] Drawing a drill location

B.] Fixing chuck on the machine spindle

C.] Removing a broken drill from the work

D.] <u>Removing the drill from the machine spindle</u>

169] When the taper shank of the drill is larger than the machine spindle, the device to hold the drill is a...

A.] Drill sleeve

B.] <u>Taper socket</u>

C.] Drill drift

D.] Chuck and key

170] The process of enlarging the end of a hole for accommodating the socket screw head is...

A.] Reaming

B.] Spot facing

C.] <u>Counter boring</u>

D.] Counter sinking

171] Appropriate tool used for spot facing operation is...

A.] Reamer

B.] Counter sinks

C.] Fly cutters

D.] Lathe tool

172] Centre drilling is an operation of...

A.] Drilling and countersinking

B.] Drilling and counter boring

C.] Marking the centre location before drilling

D.] Enlarging the diameter of a hole

173] A short reamer with an axial hole used with an arbor or mandrel is called -------

A] Parallel reamer

B] Adjustable reamer

C] Expansion reamer

D] Chucking reamer

reamer 1   Reamers

Reamer

174] Which one of the following machine reamers is used to correct the misalignment between the reamer axis and the work axis?

A] Floating blade reamer

B] Machine jig reamer.

C] Shell reamer

D] Chucking reamer

175] Tap are re sharpened by grinding -----

A] Hutes

B] Threads

C] Diameter

D] Relief

176] 50 metric coarse thread is designated as M12 x 125 What does '12' indicate?

A] Major diameter

B] Root diameter

C] Pitch diameter

D] Blank diameter

177] find the change gears required to cut a 3 mm pitch on 3 lat ' mm pitch 120

A] Driver / Driven =.455/120

B] Driver/ Driven = 60/120

C] Driver / Driven = 80/120

D] Driver/ Driven 2 40/80 of 5 mm

178] calculate the gears required to cut a 1 5 mm pitch on a lathe havmg lead screw Pitch

A] Driver / Driven -_20/100

B] Driver/ Driven = 30/100

C] Driver / Driven = 40/120

D] Driver/ Driven = 60/120

179] the top surface joining the two sides of adjacent thread is called

A] Crest

B] Root

C] Flank

D] Thread is angle

thread2   screw threads

Thread

180] The included angle of the ISO metric thread is --------

A] 27 1 /2°

B] 30°

C] 55°

D] 60°

181] Which one of the following screw thread forms has an included angle of 55° between the flanks of threads?

A] B. A. Thread

B] Acme thread

C] Buttress threads

D] Knuckle thread

182] Which one of the following is used only for finishing and maintaining correct form of thread?

A] Tap

B] Threading tool

C] Threading chaser

D] Tipped tool

183] The angle 0f lS thread (V shaped] is ----------

A] 29°

B] 47 1/4°

C] 50°

D] 60

184] ln which of the following methods, only external threads are made --------

A] Form tool mEthOd

B] Compound rest method

C] Tailstock offset method

D] Taper turning attachment method.

185] The surface joining the crest and the root of a thread is known as ----

A] Flank

B] Shank

C] Pitch surface

D] All Of these

186] Pitch of a two start thread is 4 mm. Then the lead of the thread is given by -----

A] 4mm

B] 2mm

C] 8mm

D] 6mm

187] The Gear ratio required for cutting a screw thread of 2.5 mm on a lathe having a lead screw pitch using single point cutting tool is ----

A] 1:2

B] 2:1

C] 1:1 mm

188] A die in which more than one cutting operation is per formed in one stroke

A] Piercing die

B] Progressive die

C] Combination die

D] <u>Compound die</u>

189] A die in which cutting and non cutting operations are carried out per stroke.

A] Piercing die

B] Progressive die

C] <u>Combination die</u>

D] Compound die

tap and die1   Tap Die

Tap Die

190] A die in which two or more sequential operations are performed at two or more stations upon the work.

A] Piercing die

B] <u>Progressive die</u>

C] Combination die

D] Compound die

191] A die in which the shape of the punch and die are directly reproduced in the metal with little or no metal flow.

A] Progressive die

B] Combination die

C] Compound die

D] <u>Forming die</u>

192] The die used for producing any shape of holes.

A] <u>Piercing die</u>

B] Progressive die

C] Combination die

D] Compound die

193] Abrasives are classifications into.............

A] Two types

B] Three types

c] One types

D] Four types

194] Grinding wheels made out of----------------- abrasive are most common because of its free and cool cutting action.

A] Aluminium oxide

B] Silicon oxide

C] Ammonium oxide

D] Carbide.

195] Which among the following abrasive is mostly used for cutting off wheels for cutting non metallic materials?

A] Aluminium oxide

B] Silicon carbide

C] Diamond

D] None of above

196] Which abrasive particle is used for grinding tungsten carbide tool insert?

A] Silicon carbide

B] A|203

C] Diamond

D] Corundum

197] Which of the following is the natural abrasive?

A] Aluminium oxide

B] Silicon

C] Boron carbide

D] Corundum

198] Which of the following is the manufactured abrasive?

A] Corundum.

B] Quartz

C] Silicon

D] Emery

199] Which abrasive particle is used for grinding steel fittings?

A] Silicon carbide

B] Aluminium oxide

C] Diamond.

D] boron oxide

200] What kind of abrasive cut of wheel should be used to cut concrete stone and masonry?

A] Silicon

B] Al203

C] Diamond grit

D] Glass

201] Aluminium oxide wheel is used for grinding ------------

A] cast iron

B] Cemented carbide.

C] HSS '

D] ceramic

202] The bond of diamond wheel suitable for offhand grinding of the tipped tool is ....

A] Resinoid

B] Vitrified

C] Shellac

D] Metal

Grinding wheels 1   bench grinder-wheel

Grinding Wheel

203] Which among the following bonds, is used commonly?

A] Vitrified bond '

B] Rubber bond

C] Shellac bond

D] Silicate bond

204] The symbol conventionally used for resinoid .bond is ~~~~~~~~

A] v

B] R f

C] B

D] E

205] In grinding practice the term "grade of wheel" refers to ---------'

A] Hardness of the abrasive used

B] Strength of the bond of the wheel

C] Finish 0f the Wheel

D] Hardness of the work pieces

206] Which bond is used in cut of wheels?

A] Rubber

B] Vitrified

C] Resirjoid

D] Shellac

207] Hardness of grinding wheel is determine by ----------

A] the resistance exerted. by the bond against grinding Stress

B] Hardness of abrasive grains

C] Hardness of bond

D] Ability to penetration

208] When it is required to run a Grinding wheel safely at very high speed, which bond should be used? "

A] Vitrified

B] Shellac

C] Silicate

D] resinoid' and rubber

209] in surface grinding what is the suitable range of grain size of the grinding wheel for general purpose surface grinding?

A] 20 to 36

B] 46 to 60

C] 80 to 120

D] 150 to 300

210] AS per Indian Standard, the grain '46'.comes under the group of «w. -----

A] Coarse

B] Medium

C] Fine

D] Very fine

211] The grit size of the abrasives used in the grinding wheel is usually specified by ----------

A] Hardness number
B] A size of wheel
C] Softness or hardness of the abrasive
<u>D] Mesh number</u>
212] Bench grinder are used for ....
A] Heavy duty work
B] Heavy and light duty work
<u>C] Light duty work</u>
D] Lather work
213] Bench Grinders are fitted on a ....
A] Base
<u>B] Table.</u>
C] Wheel guards
D] Conveyor
214] Which of the following statement is correct?'
<u>A] Gauges are used to check the size</u>
B] Template are used to chuck-the size
C] Gauges are used to measure the size
D] Gauges are used to check shape of component
215] At what standard temperature are the gauges kept in the section?
A] 100 C
<u>B] 20° C</u>
C] 100 F
D] 20° F
216] Which grade of slip gauge is generally used in workshop?
A] Grade 0
B] Grade l
C] Grade H
<u>D] Grade 0</u>

slip gauge 1   Slip Gauge

Slip gauge

217] As per Indian Standards a special set gauge is used consisting of
A] 81 Pieces
B] 112 Pieces
C] 120 Pieces
D] 130 Pieces
218] The accuracy of reference gauge is
A] 0.05 mm
B] 0.01 mm
C] 0.001 .
D] 0.0001 mm
219] In case of ant burr on slip gauge, it should be removed by
A] Filling
B] Lapping
C] Scraping
D] Grinding
220] Hardness of slip gauge should be?
A] More than 63 HRC
B] 58 HRC
C] 55 HRC
D] 50 HRC
221]------------- Slip gauge is used for Checking component within an accuracy of 0.01 mm.
A] Workshop gauge
B] Inspection gauge
C] Reference gauge
D] Ring gauge
222], ------------is used for checking accuracy of precision instrument.
A] Gauge block
B] Fader gauge
C] Sine bar
D] Plug gauge
223] Slip gauge are Cleaned before using to ensure accuracy. What medium will you use for this purpose.
A] Oil
B] Thinner
C] Carbon tetrachloride/ White petrol
D] Turpentine oil

224]To check the dimensional accuracy of identical components, a dial test indicator is set-for t 6 Size and used as a comparator. What will you use toset to the dial test indicator?

A] Dial test indicator

B] Teeter gauge

C] Slip gauge

D], surface gauge

225] Which one of the following is important factor required to achieve the interchange ability in mass production? .

A] Geometrical accuracy.

B] Standardization

C] Dimensional accuracy

D] Surface finish

226] Interchange ability is normally applied for? _

A] Repairing of parts

B] Mass production

C] Single piece production

D] All of these

227] When tolerance given in one side of the basic dimension, it is called ---------

A].Tolerance system

B] Unilateral tolerance

C] Bilateral tolerance

D] Allowance System

228] The measured Size Of the dimensions of a component as called----------

A] Basic size

B] Nominal Size

C] Allowed size

D] Actual size

229] In the drawing the dimensions of a shaft is shown 40i 0068/0042, which is the size of Shaft within the tolerance?

A] 4.0.64 mm

B] 40.042 mm

C] 40.000 mm

D] 39.998 mm

230] In Hole basic system ----------

A] The size of the shaft is made constant

B] The Size of the hole is made constant

C] Only 'allowance is given on the hole

D] The permissible tolerance are given on the hole and the Shaft

231] The Size of a component is given as 24 -0.1. What does -O.1 indicates? _

A] Upper deviation is + 0.1 mm .

B] Lower deviation is 0.0 mm

C] Fundamental deviation is 0.0 mm

D] Lower deviation is _0.1 mm

232] The tolerance of a hole iS the difference between the -------

A] Maximum hole Size and maximum Shaft size

B] Maximum hole size and maximum hole Size

C] Minimum'hole size and maximum Shaft Size

D] Minimum hole Size and minimum shaft Size

233] A hole whose lower deviation is zero is called basic hole. Which one of the following letter indicates basic hole?

A] E

B] F

C] G '

D] H

234] Which one having upper deviation zero?

A] Bassc Shaft

B] Basic hole

C] Tolerance

D] Clearance

235] A ball bearing on a shaft is type of fit? ,

A] Clearance fit

B] Driving fit

C] Shrinkage fit

D] None of the above

236] In the BIS system of limits and fits, the grade of tolerance are represented by number Symbols and there are ---------i

A] 14 grades of tolerance

B] 16 grades of tolerance

C] 18 grades of tolerance '

D] 20 grades of tolerance

237] A Product is said to have the quality when ....

limit fit tolarance 1

limit fit
tolerance

Limit fit tolerance

A] Its shape and dimensions are within the

B] It is fit for use

C] It appears to be very good

D] The choice of material is right

238] The maximum clearance required between hole'30 +0.021, 0.000 and shaft 30 -0.110, 0.143 is.

A] 0.110 mm '

B]0.131 mm

C] 0.164 mm

D] 0.143 mm

239] A dimension is stated as 25 .1002 mm in a drawing. What is the tolerance?

A] +0.02 mm'

B] +0.04 mm

C] -0.02 mm

D] 25.00 mm

240] A pin is fitted in a hole. The tolerance zone of the pin is entirely above that of hole. The fit obtained will be?

A] Clearance fit

B] Transition fit

C] Interference fit

D] Running fit

241] Tolerance is given to the part size to...........

A] Production the part within the required permissible size error

B] Increase the production

C] Decrease the Production

D] Finish the components approximately

242] Which one of the following is the clearance fit under the whole basic system?

A] 20 H7/p6'

B] 2067/211

C] ZOG/gll .

D] 20H/g11.

243] The three classes of fits as per BIS system aré ....

A] Clearance fit, interference fit and transition fit

B] Medium fit, push fit and tight fit

C] Flat fit, round fit and square fit

D] 'Sliding fit ', loose fit and shrinkage fit

244] Which one of the following tolerance specifications has a maximum dimensionless than 20 mm?

A] 20 +0.2,-0.3

B] 20 320.2

C] 20 -0.2, 0.3 e

D]m 20 +500, ~03

245] Difference between the maximum and minimum limit is

A] Single informant

B] Basic shaft

C] Clearance

D] Tolerance

366] Which method of development is used for developing a rectangular tray?

A] triangular method

B] radial line method

C] parallel line method

D] trial and error method

367] What is the profile of the knife cutting edge of the upper blade of the hand level shear?

A] curved

B] straight

C] inclined

D] beveled

368] For what purpose a groover is used in sheet metal work?

A] to make a hem

B] to make grooves

C] <u>to close and lock the seams</u>

D] to strength then the edge of a job

369] Which type of stake is to be selected for making sharp bends, folding of edges of sheet metal?

A] <u>hatchet stake</u>

B] beak iron stake

C] square edge stake

D] tinman's anvil stake

370] Ammonium chloride is used as a flux for soldering...

A] <u>steel</u>

B] aluminium

C] galvanized iron

D] stainless steel

371] Name the tool used to make and finish the leak proof joints of a pipe T joint

A] <u>groover</u>

B] setting hammer

C] creasing hammer

D] round bottom stake

372] Which one of the following metals will not permit X-rays to pass through?

A] stainless steel

B] aluminium

C] <u>lead</u>

D] tin

373] The frequency of up and down vibration of the cutting edge in a nibbling machine is...

A] 1000 to 1500 times

B] 1500 to 2500 times

C] <u>2800 to 3000 times</u>

D] 3000 to 3500 times

374] Name the instrument used to check the perpendicularity of the branch pipe with the main pipe of a pipe T joint

A] protractor

B] <u>try square</u>

C] spirit level

D] straight edge

375].Which type of notch is used when a single hem meets at right angles?

A] V notch

B] slit notch

C] <u>slant notch</u>

D] square notch

376] To cut out small apertures which punch and die type of machine is used?

A] shear type nibbler

B] <u>punch type nibbler</u>

C] circular cutting machine

D] guillotine shearing machine

377] The overheating of the blow pipe nozzle is to be avoided because it will

A] <u>cause back fire</u>

B] consume more oxygen and acetylene

C] create burn through defect in the joint

D] create undercut defect in the joint

378] State the nozzle size you will select to weld a 3.15mm thick mild steel sheet

A] 3

B.5

C] <u>7</u>

D] 10

379] The type of flame to be set for welding brass is...

A] air acetylene flame

B] neutral flame

C] <u>oxidizing flame</u>

D] carburizing flame

380] What is the maximum thickness of mild steel sheet recommended for gas welding using leftward technique?

A] 12mm

B] 10mm

C] 8mm

D] <u>5mm</u>

381].The distance between the root and toe of a fillet weld is called...

A] root gap

B] leg length

C] reinforcement

D] throat thickness

382] Name the weld defect which occurs due to improper cleaning of the mild steel sheet edge and surface

A] lack of root penetration

B] burn through

C] undercut

D] porosity

383] Which of the following mechanical properties of metals gives resistance to pulling forces?

A] toughness

B] ductility

C] hardness

D] tensile strength

95] If the area of a metal wire of a given length is doubles, its resistance will...

A] be doubled

B] be halved

C] remain the same

D] be four times more

96].Among the following only one is regarded as resistance wire

A] gold

B] silver

C] nichrome

D] copper

97] Arc heating occurs when the air between electrodes of opposite polarity becomes..

A] moistened

B] dry

C] ionized

D] none of the above

98] The meter used to measure the temperature of furnace is...

A] hydrometer

B] pyrometer

C] hygrometer

D] tachometer

99] in the case of electrolyte a rise in temperature causes...

A] decrease in resistance

B] increase in resistance

C] no change in resistance

D] none of the above

100] Heat developed in a conductor is proportional to the...

A] square of the power

B] square of the resistance

C] square of the current

D] square of the time

101] Out of the four metal/alloys given below, one has almost no change in resistance for temperature change...

A] nickel

B] nichrome

C] platinum

D] manganin

102] A material that is slightly repelled by a magnet is called ...

A] magnetic

B] paramagnetic

C] diamagnetic

D] ferromagnetic

103] A material that can be magnetized only very slightly is called...

A] magnetic

B] paramagnetic

C] diamagnetic

D] ferromagnetic

104] Substances that can be magnetized easily and make very strong magnets are called...

A] ferromagnetic

B] diamagnetic

C] paramagnetic

D] permanent magnetic

105] A substance that has a high retentivity can be used for the manufacture of...

A] electromagnets

B] permanent magnets

C] temporary magnets

D] paramagnets

106] A substance that has low retentivity can be used for the manufacture of...

A] <u>electromagnets</u>

B] permanent magnets

C] bar magnets

D] paramagnets

107] The symbol for inductance is...

A] H

B] I

C] <u>L</u>

D] X

108] Tube lamp choke is the best example of...

A] open circuited

B] <u>short circuited</u>

C] grounded

D] connected to the neutral line

109] The initial function of a choke in a tube light circuit is to...

A] limit the starting current

B] <u>induce high voltage</u>

C] heat up the filament

D] limit the current after starting

110] The second function of a choke in a tube light circuit is to...

A] limit the starting current

B] induce high voltage

C] heat up the filament

D] <u>limit the current after starting</u>

111] The periodic time of a wave from is 2ms] Calculate the frequency

A] 50 HZ

B] 5 HZ

C] <u>500HZ</u>

D] 5 KHZ

112] How big is the peak amplitude of a sine-wave with an effective value of 220 volts?

A] <u>311 V</u>

B] 380 V

C] 400 V

D] 440 V

113] The peak-to-peak voltage is 99V] how big is the effective value of the sine wave?

A] 70 V

B] 44.5V

C] 49.5 V

D] <u>35 V</u>

114] A moving coil voltmeter reads 10 V AC] How big is the effective voltage?

A] higher

B] lower

C] <u>the same</u>

D] 10% higher

115] A moving iron ammeter reads 10 A] how big is the peak current of the oscillation?

A] 7.07 A

B] 1.1414A

C] 70.7 A

D] <u>14.1 A</u>

116] A current of 2 amps flows through a resistance of 10 ohms] The power dissipated in the resistance is equal to...

A] 20 watts

B] 200 watts

C] <u>40 watts</u>

D] 5 watts

117] If the frequency changes from 50 HZ to 100 HZ keeping voltage constant, the inductive reactance of coil connected to supply...

A] remains same

B] become half

C] <u>become doubled</u>

D] become 4 times

118] Capacitance is not affected by...

A] plate area

B] distance between plates

C] dialectic material

D] <u>frequency</u>

119] The capacitive reactance of a capacitor varies...

A] directly with frequency

B] <u>inversely with frequency</u>

C] directly with applied voltage

D] inversely with applied voltage

120] A capacitor acquired 3 coulombs of charge when 6 volts are applied across it] It has a capacitance of ...

A] 0.5 farad

B] 3 farads

C] 3 farads

D] 18 farads

121] A capacitor is connected across a 200 volt AC line, its minimum voltage rating should be...

A] 100 volts

B] 200 Volts

C] 300 volts

D] 400 volts

122] when testing a capacitor with an ohmmeter, the meter indicates some resistance] The capacitor under test is...

A] leaky

B] open

C] good

D] short

123] The total capacitance of a 40 micro farad capacitor connected in series with an 80 micro farad capacitor is...

A] 26.7 micro farad

B] 40 micro farad

C] 60.6 micro farad

D] 120 micro farad

124] For obtaining 1 micro farad capacitor from 3 nos] of 3 micro farad capacitors we have to connect...

A] all in parallel

B] all in series

C] 2 series and one in parallel

D] none of the above

125] In an AC series circuit having R and C the current flowing through the capacitor will be...

A] lagging the voltage

B] leading the voltage

C] in phase with the voltage

D] none of the above

126] If the frequency of the supply is increased in the R-C series circuit the capacitive reactance will be

A] reduced

B] increased

C] having no effect

D] none of the above

127] Power companies are interested in improving the power factor to

A] reduce line current

B] increase motor efficiency

C] increase volt-amperes

D] decrease power

128] A capacitor increases the power factor value of an AC motor load when it is connected...

A] in series with the motor

B] in series with the starter

C] in parallel with the motor

D] in series with the main winding

129] Normally, the power factor of an incandescent lighting circuit is..

A] 0

B] 0.5

C] 0.707

D] 1.0

130] When resistance alone is used to determine current in an RLC series circuit, the circuit is...

A] an inductive circuit

B] a capacitive circuit

C] a combination circuit

D] a resonant circuit

131] Inductive reactance is directly related to..

A] resistance

B] frequency

C] capacitance

D] power

132] Synchronous motor when used for power factor improvement should be...

A] under excited

B] over excited

C] loaded

D] running at no load

133] In a RL parallel circuit, the opposition to total current is called...

A] reactance

B] resistance

C] a vector sum

D] <u>impedance</u>

134] In a AC parallel RL circuit, the power dissipated at the

A] impedance

B] <u>resistance</u>

C] inductance

D] capacitance

135] How much is the nominal output voltage of a carbon zinc cell?

A] 12V

B] <u>1.5V</u>

C] 2.0V

D] 2.2V

136] Cells are connected in series to..

A] <u>increase the output voltage</u>

B] decreases the output voltage

C] decrease the internal resistance

D] increase the current capacity

54137connected in

A] series

B] <u>parallel</u>

C] series-parallel

D] parallel-series

138] The capacity of a cell is measured in

A] watt-hour

B] watts

C] amperes

D] <u>ampere-hour</u>

139] The primary cell which has the shortest shelf life is

A] <u>carbon – zinc</u>

B] alkaline

C] mercury

D] lithium

140] The cell which has very high energy density for given weight or volume to

A] carbon-zinc
B] alkaline
C] mercury
D] lithium

141] A 100-Ah capacity battery should deliver a current of 8A for approximately...
A] 12 h
B] 8 h
C] 20 h
D] 100 h

142] When the battery is needed to be kept idle for a long time...
A] overcharge the battery
B] remove electrolyte
C] clean the plates with distilled water
D] dry them and store the battery in cool dry clean place

143] The active materials of the nickel iron cell are...
A] nickel hydroxide
B] powdered iron and its oxide
C] 21% solution of caustic potash
D] all the above materials

144] The capacity of a cell is measured in
A] watt hour
B] watts
C] amperes
D] ampere-hour

145] To charge a secondary cell, the system used is
A] low voltage AC
B] high voltage AC
C] AC
D] DC

187] If the thin cables are used for starter motor
A] Cable wilt get heated up
B] Voltage drop
C] Supply lesser current
D] Supply more current.

188] The main feed wires from the battery consists the main colour of
A] White
B] Brown.

D] red
D] Black
189] Earth circuit colour
C] Blue/red
D] Red
E] Black
F] White
190] Front parking lamp colour
A] Brown
B] Yellow
C] Blue/red
D] Red
191] ignition circuit colour
C] Blue/red
D] Red
E] Black
F] White
192] Generating circuit colour
A] Brown
B] Yellow
C] Blue/red
D] Red
193] Head light circuit colour
A] Brown
B] Yellow
C] Blue/red
D] Red
194] Battery feed circuit colour
A] Brown
B] Yellow
C] Blue/red
D] Red

lead acid battery6   electric-car-battery

Lead acid battery in vehicle

195] Measures voltage of battery
A] Resistance
B] <u>Voltmeter</u>
C] Ammeter
D] Cell tester
250] Fluid under pressures
A] To start heavy duty engine
B] Starter motor
C] <u>Hydraulic cranking</u>
D] Electric motor
251] Hydraulic floor jack is used
A] To remove king pin bush
B] <u>To lift the wheel</u>
C] To press the bush
D] Hold the job.
252] Which one of the following is the advantage of pneumatic system?
A] For low cost layout
B] For increasing the rate of production
C] For better working environment
D] <u>All of these</u>
253]The pressure of fluid in hydraulic brake system is governed by
A] boils law
B] Charles law
C] <u>Pascal's law</u>
D] none of the above laws
254] Allows fluid both way in and out of cylinder

A] Piston
B] Push Rod
C] Primary cup
D] <u>Check valve</u>
255] Seals the compensating port
A] Piston
B] Push Rod
C] <u>Primary cup</u>
D] Check valve
256] Actuates the piston
A] Piston
B] <u>Push Rod</u>
C] Primary cup
D] Check valve
257] Develops pressure on fluid
A] <u>Piston</u>
B] Push Rod
C] Primary cup
D] Check valve
258] Develops pressure on fuel to go out
A] Valves
B] Coil spring
C] <u>Diaphragm</u>
D] Rocker arm
259] Actuates the diaphragm
A] Valves
B] Coil spring
C] Diaphragm
D] <u>Rocker arm</u>
268] In diesel cycle Combustion takes place at
A] <u>Constant pressure</u>
B] Constant volume' '
C] Constant temperature
D] Constant temperature and pressure.
269] Rudolf Diesel, developed a Cl.engine
A] 1876
B] 1880
C] <u>1892</u>

D] 1930

engines5

diesel engine-valves

Engine in vehicle

270] Perkins built 'P' series engines
A] 1876
B] 1880
C] 1892
D] <u>1930</u>
271] N.A OTTO developed a 4 stroke cycle engine
A] <u>1876</u>
B] 1880
C] 1892

D] 1930
272] Dugald Clerk developed a 2 stroke cycle engine
A] 1876
B] <u>1880</u>
C] 1892
D] 1930
273] All cylinders in a horizontal line
A] 'V' Engine
B] <u>Inline Engine</u>
C] Opposed Engine
D] Radial Engine
274] Cylinders positioned in 'V' shape
A] <u>'V' Engine</u>
B] Inline Engine
C] Opposed Engine
D] Radial Engine
275] Cylinders positioned radially
A] 'V' Engine
B] Inline Engine
C] Opposed Engine
D] <u>Radial Engine</u>
276] Cylinders arranged horizontally opposite to each other
A] 'V' Engine
B] Inline Engine
C] <u>Opposed Engine</u>
D] Radial Engine
293] What IS the reason for hissing noise from cylinder head?
A] excessive tappet clearance
B] wrong injection timing
C] pie-ignition
D] <u>air cleaner mounting loose.</u>
294] Mounted on cylinder head or block
A] Fins
B] Radiators
C] Fan
D] <u>Water pump</u>
295] Allows fluid both way in and out of cylinder
A] Piston

B] Push Rod
C] Primary cup
D] <u>Check valve</u>
296] Relieves excess pressure of air from the air tank.
A] Air compressor
B] Unloader valve
C] <u>Safety valve</u>
D] Brake chamber

air tank safety valve

mmv air tank safety valve

Air tank safety valve

297] Regulates maximum air pressure, reaching to air tank.
A] Air compressor
B] <u>Unloader valve</u>
C] Safety valve
D] Brake chamber
298] Supplies air to front and rear brake
A] Brake actuator
B] <u>Dual brake valve</u>
C] System protection valve
D] Flick valve

hydraulic pnumatic
brakes
brakes

Brakes in car

299] Operated for parking the vehicle.
A] Brake actuator
B] Dual brake valve
C] System protection valve
D] <u>Flick valve</u>
300] Distributes air to various circuits
A] Brake actuator
B] Dual brake valve
C] <u>System protection valve</u>
301] Keeps valves in closed position
A] Push Rod
B] Tappet
C] <u>Spring</u>
D] Cam lobe

engine valves3

diesel engine-valves

Engine valves

302] Allow fuel to flow in and out
A] <u>Valves</u>
B] Coil spring
C] Diaphragm
D] Rocker arm

cooling system3

engine cooling

Cooling system in car

303] Allows coolants into the expansion tank

A] <u>Pressure relief valve</u>

B] Engine fan belt

C] Radiator drain plug

D] Over flow pipe

304] An overflow valve is used

A] <u>to send back excess fuel from the fuel filler</u>

B] to supply more fuel to the fuel filter

C] to supply clean fuel

D]to take the leaking fuel

305] Feed pumps are driven by

A] camshaft of engine

B] <u>Camshaft of FIP</u>

C] Timing Gears

D] Varies from engine to engine.

306] The oil pumps are generally driven by

A] <u>camshaft</u>

B] rocker shaft

C] crankshaft

D] damper pulley

307]Engine develops less power due to

A]<u>defective ignition timing</u>

B]excessive rich mixture

C]defective lubrication system

D]too tight cylinder head

308] Creates pressure on fluid

A] Brake pedal

B] <u>Master cylinder piston</u>

C] Wheel cylinder piston

D] Distribution block

309] Pushes master cylinder piston through linkages.

A] <u>Brake pedal</u>

B] Master cylinder piston

C] Wheel cylinder piston

D] Distribution block

310] Actuates the piston

A] Piston

B] <u>Push Rod</u>

C] Primary cup

D] Check valve

311] Develops pressure on fluid

A] <u>Piston</u>

B] Push Rod

C] Primary cup

D] Check valve

piston rings & valves7   diesel-engine-piston-rings

Piston & rings in Engine

312] Displacement volume of piston

A] |.H.P.

B] <u>Swept volume</u>

C] Mechanical efficiency

D] Horse power

313] Starting point of piston's downward movement in the cylinder

A] <u>T.D.C.</u>

B] Cycle

C] B.D.C.

D] Ignition

314] Starting point of piston's upward movement in the cylinder

A] T.D.C.

B] Cycle

C] <u>B.D.C.</u>

D] Ignition

315] Prevents blow by

A] Piston

B] Piston pin

C] Connecting rod

D] <u>Piston rings</u>

316] Reciprocates in the cylinder

A] <u>Piston</u>

B] Piston pin

C] Connecting rod

D] Piston rings

317] Connects piston and connecting rod
A] Piston
B] <u>Piston pin</u>
C] Connecting rod
D] Piston rings

318] Oscillates in cylinder
A] Piston
B] Piston pin
C] <u>Connecting rod</u>
D] Piston rings

319]The top and bottom halves of connecting rod are bolted on
A] crankshaft man journal
B] <u>crankpin journal</u>
C] camshaft
D] piston pin boss

320] A hole is drilled between crankshaft main journal and crank pin for
A] balancing of crankshaft
B] reducing crankshaft weight
C] <u>lubricating connecting rod bearings</u>
D] reducing crankshaft vibrations

321] Converts reciprocating motion into rotary motion
A] <u>Crankshaft</u>
B] Flywheels
C] Torque wrench
D] Thrust bearing

322] Rotary movement to pull and push action
A] Wiper motor
B] <u>Cranking link</u>
C] **Pinion**
D] Wiper blade

323] Accommodates wheel hub bearings.
A] Kingpin
B] Spring pad
C] <u>Stub axle shaft portion</u>
D] Track rod ball joints

324] Pushes with drawal plate
A] Clutch cover
B] <u>Release bearing</u>

C] Release fingers
D] Clutch plate
325] **Takes thrust load**
A] Crankshaft
B] Flywheels
C] Torque wrench
D] <u>Thrust bearing</u>
326]Distributor shaft is supported by
A] ball bearing
B] shell bearing
C] <u>bush bearing</u>
D] needle bearing
327] Stores energy
A] Crankshaft
B] <u>Flywheels</u>
C] Torque wrench
D] Thrust bearing
328] engages with the flywheel ring
A] <u>Pinion</u>
B] Over running clutch
C] Plunger disk
D] Clutch
329] Flywheel magneto consists of
A] Temporary magnet
B] Bar magnet
C] <u>Permanent magnet</u>
D] Needle magnet.
330] in flywheel magneto, the ignition coil is
A] <u>stationary</u>
B] Moving
C] Rotating
D] Oscillating.
331] To rotate the permanent magnet
A] Switch
B] Secondary coils
C]<u>Flywheels</u>
D] Condensers
332] While reversing the vehicle the driver should control

A] <u>Clutch</u>
B] Forward gear
C] Accelerator
D] Hand brake.
333] The clutch plate assembly has a centre steel disc riveted with springs for
A] strength
B] flexibility
C] less noise
D] <u>absorbing shocks</u>
334] Dog clutches are used in
A] <u>gear boxes</u>
B] friction clutches
C] brakes
D] differentials

dog clutches2

mmv dog clutches

Dog clutches in vehicle
335] Synchromesh mechanisms is provided for
A] Increasing the speed of the vehicle
B] Reducing the speed of the vehicle

C] <u>Smooth gear engagement'</u>

D] None of the above.

336] Only spur gears are used

A] <u>Sliding mesh</u>

B] Synchromesh

C] Double declutching

D] Transfer case

337] Used for smooth gear shifting

A] Sliding mesh

B] Synchromesh

C] Double <u>declutching</u>

D] Transfer case

338] Hard gear shifting is due to

A] Worn out clutch disc

B] Damaged main shaft bearings

C] <u>Synchronizer unit damaged</u>

D] Excessive oil in the gearbox.

339] Gear slip is due to

A] <u>Worn out synchroniser</u>

B] Worn out clutch disc

C] Dry main shaft bearing

D] Weak pressure spring of clutch.

340] Noise in particular gear is due to

A] Insufficient clutch pedal free play

B] Damage gear teeth

C] Cracked gear box case

D] <u>Damaged synchromesh unit</u>.

341] Gearshift lever is used for

A] Releasing clutch

B] <u>Changing gear</u>

C] Increasing the speed of the engine

D] Controlling the direction of vehicle.

steering gearbox3   steering system

Steering gearbox in vehicle

342] In which type of steering gear box variable steering ration is achieved?

A] <u>worm and roller steering gear</u>

B] worm and nut steering gear

C] worm and sector steering gear

D] rack and pinion steering gear

speed gear box6

gear box

Speed gear box in vehicle

343] The vehicle attains different speed by means of

A] <u>gear box</u>

B] clutch

C] differential

D] rear axle & wheel

344] Dog clutches are used in

A] <u>gear boxes</u>

B] friction clutches

C] brakes

D] differentials

345] in a 3 speed gear box in following combination of gears are provided

A] <u>3 forward and 1 reverse</u>

B] 2 forward and 1 reverse

C] 4 forward

D] 2 forward and 2 reverse

346] which gear does not produce axial trust

A] <u>spur gear</u>

B] helical gear

C] spiral bevel gear

D] bevel gear

347] which gears converts rotary motion into linear motion

A] worm gears

B] herring bone gear

C] <u>rack & pinion</u>

D] helical gear

348] What is a reason for gear slip

A] unlubricated gear linka-ges

B] less oil in gear box

C] broken teeth of gear

D] <u>wrong adjustment of gear lever</u>

350]The boiling temperature of the coolant in the cooling in the cooling system is increased by the use of

A]water jackets

B]vacuum valve only

C]<u>pressure type radiator cap</u>

D] radiator core tubes/pipes

radiator cap4   mmv Radiator cap

Radiator cap in vehicle

351] The main purpose of pressure radiator cap is to

A]pressurize the system

B]increase air water circulation

C]help to develop vacuum in the system

D]avoid build up to pressure

352] one of the following causes may also contribute to overheating of an engine

A]clogged radiator cores

B]low idle speed setting

C]excessive valve tappet clearance

D]lubricating oil pressure is too high

353] Mounted on cylinder head or block

A] Fins

B] Radiators

C] Fan

D] Water pump

354] Drives the water pump

A] Pressure relief valve

B] Engine fan belt

C] Radiator drain plug

D] Over flow pipe

355] If thermostat valve remains in an open position then which of the following will happen

A]slow warming up to engine

B]engine will over heat

C]engine fails to start

D]stalling of engine

thermostat valve

thermostat

Thermostat valve in vehicle

356]In a dry sump lubrication system, a scavenging pump is used to

A] <u>pump oil from sump to tank</u>

B] pump oil directly to all moving parts

C] develop additional oil pressure

D] pump oil from tank to sum

357]Excessive oil pressure in the lubrication system may be due to

A] less quantity of engine oil in sump

B] <u>incorrect adjustment of relief valve</u>

C] less suction effect on the suction pipe

D] none of the above

358] Which component among the following reduces noise of exhaust gases?

A] Exhaust pipe

B] Muffler

C] <u>inlet manifold</u>

D] tail pipe.

359] Air compressor's driven by

A] To start heavy duty engine

B] Starter motor

C] Hydraulic cranking

D] <u>Electric motor</u>

360] Provides compressed air to system

A] <u>Air compressor</u>

B] Unloader valve

C] Safety valve

D] Brake chamber

361] Air compressors is used for

A] <u>Multipurpose</u>

B] To lift the car only

C] To lift and remove the wheel

D] To grind the chisel.

362] in the air compressor, the safety device is used to

A] To suck the air

B] To release the air completely

C] To regulate the air pressure

D] <u>To release excess air pressure</u>.

363] Used in air compressor

A] <u>Pressure gauge</u>

B] Oil tank

C] Oil spray gun

D] Car hoist

364] Cleans the air entering the cylinder

A] Air horn

B] Fuel bowl

C] <u>Air cleaner</u>

D] Air bleed

382] Moving coil instrument works on the effect of...

A] chemical effect

B] heating effect

C] electrostatic effect

D] <u>electromagnetic effect</u>

383] Battery power
A] To start heavy duty engine
B] <u>Starter motor</u>
C] Hydraulic cranking
D] Electric motor

starter winding

armature2   mmv Starter winding armature

Starter winding armature in vehicle

384] connect two terminals of solenoid.
A] Pinion
B] Over running clutch
C] <u>Plunger disk</u>
D] Clutch

385] When the horn button is pressed the current flows to horn through
A] Horn switch
B] <u>Solenoid coil</u>
C] Battery
D] Chassis.

386] Turns core to magnet
A] <u>Solenoid Switch</u>
B] Actuating wire (when heated]
C] Ballast Resistors
D] Actuating wire (when cooled]

387] The alternator in a car delivers 4A and has a load of 3 ohms connected across its terminals. Find the voltage of the circuit
A] 18V

B] 24V

C] <u>12V</u>

D] 16V

388 Which type of steering system used in bulldozer?

A] Wheel type

B] Pedal type

C] <u>Stick type</u>

D] Handle bar type

2 Which type of vehicle provides separate steering for left and right wheel tracks?

A] Tractor

B] Jeep

C] Tipper

D] <u>Bulldozer</u>

3 Which electrical device rotate the flywheel of tractor engine?

A] Alternator

B] <u>Starter motor</u>

C] Battery

D] Wiper motor

4 Which type of cranking system is used to crank the heavy duty multicylinder diesel engine?

A] Compressed air cranking

B] <u>Gasoline engine cranking</u>

C] Handle cranking

D] Rope cranking

1. Power tiller is a ______________

a) <u>Prime mower</u>

b) Orchard mower

c) Small tractor

d) Garden tractor

2. Which of the following country uses more power tiller?

a) India

b) <u>Japan</u>

c) Russia

d) America

3. In India, the introduction of power tiller was in?

a) <u>1963</u>

b) 1950

c) 1940

d) 1981

4. The kerosene oil operate power is ___________

a) Kubota

b) Krishi

c) <u>Iseski</u>

d) Mitsubishi

5. In power tiller, the power is obtained from ___________

a) I.C. engine

b) <u>Power rim</u>

c) Gasoline

d) Coal

6. In power tiller, the tilling attachment receives the power from ______

a) <u>Main clutch</u>

b) Tilling clutch

c) PTO

d) Transmission gear

7. In bigger power tillers, the type of main clutch used is ___________

a) <u>Friction clutch</u>

b) Rubber clutch

c) V-belt clutch

d) Leather clutch

8. In power tillers, the most commonly used brake is ___________

a) Inner side expansion type

b) <u>Friction type</u>

c) Shoe type

d) Rubber plate type

9. In power tiller, the steering clutch lever is possible ___________

a) <u>On the grip of right and left handles</u>

b) On right handle

c) On left handle

d) In front of driver seat

10. Useful life of power tiller is ___________

a) <u>10 years</u>

b) 15 years

c) 5 years

d) 2 years

11. The HP of ISEKI made power tiller is ___________

a) <u>8</u>

b) 7

c) 5-7

d) 9

12. In power tiller for transmitting the power from engine to the main clutch the belt used is ___________

a) <u>V-belt</u>

b) Leather belt

c) Canvas belt

d) Flat belt

13. In power tiller, the wheel receives the power from __________

a) Tilting clutch

b) <u>Steering clutch</u>

c) Main clutch

d) PTO

14. In power tiller, the engine transmits the power first to __________

a) <u>Main clutch</u>

b) Wheels

c) Steering clutch

d) Transmission gear

INDUSTRIAL TRAINING INSTITUTE

Monthly Test-1, Marks- 20, Date:- _______________

(Every Question Carry Two Marks)

01] In case of bleeding, take treatment Of

A] spray cold water

B] Bandage immediately -----]

C] Enquire about the accident thought treatment

D] cold 3" and rest

02] in case of an accident, the victim should im

A] Asked to take rest

C] Attended immediately

D] leave him

03] First aid is given to an injured or ill person primarily....

A] Save life

B] Prevent further deterioration of the muff's

C] Give best possible comfort

D] All of these

04] Colour code for Bins for waste paper segregation is -----

A] blue Colour

B] Yellow Colour

C] Red Colour

D] Green Colour

05] In Japanese Seiko stands for --------------

A] Shine

B] Sort

C] Standardize

D] Sustain

06] Benefit of SS system is ------

A] Increase in productivity

B] Increase in quality

C] Reduction in wastage of time

D] All of these

07] Safety is -----------

A] nobody's business

B] every bodise business

C] Some bodies business

D] The organization business

08] For basic categories of safety signs are available The meaning of"prohibition" sign ----

A] shows it must not be done

B] Shows what must be done

C] Warns the hazard or danger

D] Gives information of safety provision

09] Which one is a workshop safety?

A] Keep shop floor clean and free from grease, oil or other slippery materials

B] Stop the machine before changing the speed

C] Don't use cracked or chipped tools

D] Don't try to stop a running machine with hand

10] In Personal Protect Equipment (PPE] HELMET is used to

A] protect head

B] Protect eyes

C] Protect hands

D] Protect ears

INDUSTRIAL TRAINING INSTITUTE

Monthly Test-2, Marks- 20, Date:- _______________

(Every Question Carry Two Marks)

1- 17] Which type of fire extinguisher is used to put off general fire?

A] Water type Extinguisher

B] Foam type Extinguisher

C] Dry chemical powder Extinguisher

D] Carbon dioxide (C02] Extinguisher

2-18] One micrometer (U] is equal to...

A] 0.1mm

B] 0.01mm

C] 0.001mm

D] 0.0001mm

3-19] Name the tool used to make and finish the leak proof joints of a pipe T joint

A] groover

B] setting hammer

C] creasing hammer

D] round bottom stake

4-20] Portion of the hammer used for fixing the handle is...

A] Face

B] Peen

C] Cheek

D] Eye hole

5-21] Weight of the hammer for the marking purpose is...

A] 250g

B] 500g

C] 1 kg

D] 2 kgs

6-22] To cut out small apertures which punch and die type of machine is used?

A] shear type nibbler

B] punch type nibbler

C] circular cutting machine

D] guillotine shearing machine

7-23] Scribers are made of...

A] Mild steel

B] High carbon steel

C] Brass

D] Cast iron

8-24] The size of an engineer's vice is specified by the...

A] Length of the movable jaw

B] Width of the jaws

C] Height of the vice

D] Maximum opening of the jaws

9-25] The form of thread used in carpenters vice is...

A] Square

B] Acme thread

C] Sawtooth Thread

D] Knuckle thread

10-26] The convexity of files helps...

A] To file concave surfaces

B] To file convex surfaces

C] To prevent rounding of edges of work

D] The file to become straight when pressure is applied

INDUSTRIAL TRAINING INSTITUTE

Monthly Test-3, Marks- 20, Date:- _______________

(Every Question Carry Two Marks)

1-33] The reason for using cast iron in making 'V' blocks

A] to increase the weight of the block

B] to reduce the cost

C] to reduce the friction

D] to get a good appearance

2-34] For cutting thin tubing, the most suitable pitch of the hacksaw blade is...

A] 1.8mm

B] 1.4mm

C] 1mm

D] 0.8mm

3-35] For cutting solid brass, the most suitable pitch of the hacksaw blade is...

A] 1.8mm

B] 1.4mm

C] 1mm

D] 0.8mm

4-36] A new hacksaw blade after a few strokes becomes loose because of the...

A] Stretching of the blade

B] Wing-nut threads being worn out

C] Wrong pitch of the blade

D] Improper selection of the set of saws.

5-37] While cutting small diameter pipes, it is advisable to watch regularly and ensure that...

A] The cut is along the curved line

B] More saw teeth are in contract

C] The work is not overheated

D] Proper balancing of hacksaw is maintained

6-38] If the drill runs untrue, it will

A] get too hot

B] cut undersize

C] distort the spindle

D] cut an oversized hole

7-39] Running the drill too fast many result in

A] spoiling the cutting edge

B] poor surface finish

C] twisting the tang

D] drilling an oval hole

8-40] A drill with worn land will

A] drill hole oversize

B] drill hole undersize

C] run out of centre

D] drill an accurate hole

9-41] The morse taper provided on drills used on lathe ranges between

A] MT1 to MT5

B] MT1 to MT4

C] MT0 to MT5

D] MT0 to MT4

10-42] Feeding the small drill too fast into the work may result in

A] breaking the drill

B] bending the drill

C] cutting an oval shape hole

D] increased production

INDUSTRIAL TRAINING INSTITUTE

Monthly Test-4, Marks- 20, Date:- _______________

(Every Question Carry Two Marks)

1-50] The point angle of drills depends on...

A] The size of the drill

B] The type of machine

C] <u>The material of the work</u>

D] The RPM of the drill

2-51] The point angle for a standard drill is...

A] 60°

B] 108°

C] <u>118°</u>

D] 135°

3-52] The helical angle determines the...

A] Cutting angle

B] Chew angle

C] <u>Rake angle</u>

D] Lip angle

4-53] The clearance angle of the drill is between...

A] 3° to 5°

B] <u>8° to 12°</u>

C] 12° to 20°

D] 15° to 20°

5-54] The relief angle provided behind the cutting edge is called the..

A] Point angle

B] Chisel edge angle

C] Helix angle

D] <u>Clearance angle</u>

6-55] A set of number drill series consists of drills in the following ranges] Indicate the correct range

A] 1 to 40

B] 1 to 50

C] <u>1 to 80</u>

D] 1 to 100

7-56] In the number drill series, the smallest drill size is...

A] 0.1 mm

B] <u>0.35 mm</u>

C] 0.5 mm

D] 0.52 mm

8-57] In the number drill series, the largest drill size is...

A] 102 mm

B] <u>5.791 mm</u>

C] 5.613 mm

D] 5.410 mm

9-58] In the letter drill series, the size of the drill 'A' is equal to ...

A] 13 mm

B] 6.08 mm

C] 6.045 mm

D] <u>5.944 mm</u>

10-59] In the letter drill series, the largest drill size is equal to...

A] 10.33 mm

B] <u>10.490 mm</u>

C] 12.01 mm

D] 15.00 mm

INDUSTRIAL TRAINING INSTITUTE
Monthly Test-5, Marks- 20, Date:- ________________
(Every Question Carry Two Marks)

1-66] which one of the following is the most suitable tap for lathe work?

A] spiral tap

B] machine tap

C] hand tap

D] left hand tap

2-67] A die is turned with a

A] die wrench

B] diestock

C] die plate

D] die handle

3-68] A tumbler gear unit has

A] a single gear

B] two gears

C] three gears

D] four gears

4-69] The cutting edge of a solid tool is made of

A] carbon steel

B] mild steel

C] super high speed steel

D] stelite

5-70] The tip of a cemented carbide threading tool is

A] brazed

B] welded

C] soldered

D] clamped to the shank

6-71] Tool will rub against the work surfaces and the cutting force increases when..

A] The clearance angle is more

B] The clearance angel is less

C] The rake angle is more

D] The rake angle is less

7-72] Formation of a chip while cutting is based on the...

A] Rake angle of the tool

B] Clearance angle of the tool

C] Wedge angle of the tool

D] Clearance and wedge angle of the tool

8-73] The suitable cutting fluid for drilling mild steel in a drilling machine is...

A] Synthetic soluble oil

B] Neat oil

C] Distilled water

D] Soluble oil

9-74] Centre drilling is an operation of...

A] Drilling and countersinking

B] Drilling and counter boring

C] Marking the centre location before drilling

D] Enlarging the diameter of a hole

10-75] Shaft ends are centre drilled for...

A] Supporting jobs between centres

B] Lubricating the dead centre

C] Reducing the weight

D] Assisting counter boring

INDUSTRIAL TRAINING INSTITUTE

Monthly Test-6, Marks- 20, Date:- _______________

(Every Question Carry Two Marks)

1-80] The process of enlarging the end of a hole for accommodating the socket screw head is...

A] Reaming

B] Spot facing

C] Counter boring

D] Counter sinking

2-81]While choosing a boring tool for boring a given diameter, select

A] a long tool

B] a short tool

C] a long and stout tool

D] a short and stout tool

3-82] The cutting edge of the boring tool should be set for a small hole so that it is

A] 0.5 mm above the center

B] 0.5 mm below the center

C] 1 mm above the center

D] in the exact center

4-83] Bored holes are to be chamfered by using

A] a drill

B] triangular scraper

C] a cranked boring tool

D] a flat file

5-84] The tool used for boring deep holes is a

A] lathe mandrel

B] sleeve

C] drill

D] auger bit

6-85] The cutting speed for rough boring is the

A] same as rough turning

B] same as drilling

C] same as knurling

D] same as thread cutting

7-86] The reamer is used for...

A] Drilling holes in thin sheets

B] Drilling deep holes

C] Removing burrs

D] Enlarging and finishing holes

8-87] The reamer teeth are unevenly spaced because...

A] They are easy to manufacture

B] They can reduce chattering

C] They help to cut metal gradually

D] They help to remove the reamer easily

9-88] Which among the following is not a capability of reamers?

A] Finishing small holes

B] Finishing any machined profiles

C] Accuracy to closer limits

D] Producing high quality surface finish

10-89] The most important quality of any cutting fluid is

A] emulsification

B] specific heat

C] specific gravity

D] viscosity

INDUSTRIAL TRAINING INSTITUTE

Monthly Test-7, Marks- 20, Date:- _______________

(Every Question Carry Two Marks)

1-95] The depth of cut is given by

A] the top slide

B] the cross-slide

C] the compound slide

D] adjusting the tool

2-96] For mounting a lathe chuck

A] start it by hand and then turn the power on

B] mount it on by power

C] mount it by hand

D] mount it with the help of a hammer

3-97] The morse taper provided on drills used on lathe ranges between

A] MT1 to MT5

B] MT1 to MT4

C] MT0 to MT5

D] MT0 to MT4

4-98] Feeding the small drill too fast into the work may result in

A] breaking the drill

B] bending the drill

C] cutting an oval shape hole

D] increased production

5-99] Number of flutes in a twist drills are --------

A] 1

B] 2

C] 3

D] 4

6-100] Which one of the following drilling machines is used for drilling holes where electricity is not available?

A] Bench drilling machine

B] Pillar drilling machine

C] Redial drilling machine

D] Ratchet drilling machine

7-101] Which one of the following drilling machine is used for heavy duty work?

A] Bench drilling machine

B] Pillar drilling machine

C] Radial drilling machine

D] Electric hand drilling machine

8-102] The suitable cutting fluid for drilling mild steel in a lathe is

A] synthetic soluble oil

B] neat cutting oil

C] distilled water

D] soluble oil+water

9-103] The suitable cutting fluid for precision grinding is

A] Soluble oil

B] Synthetic soluble oil

C] Neat oil

D] Servo Cut's'

10-104] Advantage of using cutting fluid during grinding operation is ------

A] 5000 surface finish

B] Reduction in cutting forces

C] Reduction in hardening of the work piece

D] All of these]

INDUSTRIAL TRAINING INSTITUTE

Monthly Test-8, Marks- 20, Date:- ______________

(Every Question Carry Two Marks)

1-110] Which is correct angle plate used with face plate

(A] Solid Type

(B] Box Type

(C] Adjustable Type

(D] None of them

2-111] Face plate is made from.....]

(A] Mild Steel

(B] Cast Iron

(C] Brass

(D] Aluminium

3-112] Which following accessories is use for odd an uneven job turning?

(A] Three Jaw Chuck

(B] Two Jaw Chuck

(C] Driving Plate

(D] Face Plate

4-113] An irregular shaped work piece is turned on a Lathe] Which one of the following work holding accessories is used?

A] Two Jaw chuck

B] Three Jaw chuck

C] Driving plate

D] Face plate

5-114]The pads of a steady rest are made of

A] carbon steel

B] lead

C] mild steel

D] brass

6-115] A steady rest is used

A] to hold jobs

B] for face plate work

C] to drive the job

D] to support the job

7-116] A follower steady is held on the

A] lathe bed

B] lathe carriage

C] lathe spindle

D] tailstock

8-117] When turning long work pieces, the following is used

A sleeve

B change gear

C steady rest

D bracket]

9-118] Knurling operation is done at the

A] turning spindle speed

B] high spindle speed

C] 1/3 of the turning spindle speed

D] 1⁄2 of the turning spindle speed

10-119] Knurling is the operation of

A] shearing

B] forming

C] turning

D] pressing

INDUSTRIAL TRAINING INSTITUTE

Monthly Test-9, Marks- 20, Date:- _______________

(Every Question Carry Two Marks)

1-125] The number of fundamental deviations in the B.I.S] system are

A] 20

B] 22

C] 25

D] 28

2-126] The number of grade of tolerances in the B.I.S] system are

A] 12

B] 16

C] 18

D] 20

**3-127] The size based on which the dimensional deviations are given
is called...**

A] Actual size

B] Basic size

C] Minimum limit of size

D] Maximum limit of Size

**4-128] The size of parts made by .....] for provide interchange ability
properties] (A] Measurement System**

(B] Trial and Error System

(C] Limit and Tolerance System

(D] None of Them

5-129] Your job taper is correct if it is measured

A above the higher limit

B in between higher and lower limit

C below the lower limit]

6-130] When tolerance given in one side of the basic dimension, it is called --------

A].Tolerance system

B] Unilateral tolerance

C] Bilateral tolerance

D] Allowance System

7-131] A dimension is stated as (025 H7 in a drawing] The lower limit is -----------

A] 24.75 mm

B] 24.85 mm

C] 25.00 mm

D] 25-021 mm

8-132] The measured Size Of the dimensions of a component as called---------

A] Basic size

B] Nominal Size

C] Allowed size

D] Actual size

9-133] In the drawing the dimensions of a shaft is shown 40i 0068/ 0042, which is the size of Shaft within the tolerance?

A] 4.0.64 mm

B] 40.042 mm

C] 40.000 mm

D] 39.998 mm

10-134] In Hole basic system ----------

A] The size of the shaft is made constant

B] The Size of the hole is made constant

C] Only 'allowance is given on the hole

INDUSTRIAL TRAINING INSTITUTE

Monthly Test-10, Marks- 20, Date:- _______________

(Every Question Carry Two Marks)

268] In diesel cycle Combustion takes place at

A] Constant pressure

B] Constant volume' '

C] Constant temperature

D] Constant temperature and pressure.

269] Rudolf Diesel, developed a Cl.engine

A] 1876

B] 1880

C] 1892

D] 1930

270] Perkins built 'P' series engines

A] 1876

B] 1880

C] 1892

D] 1930

271] N.A OTTO developed a 4 stroke cycle engine

A] 1876

B] 1880

C] 1892

D] 1930

272] Dugald Clerk developed a 2 stroke cycle engine

A] 1876

B] 1880

C] 1892

D] 1930

273] All cylinders in a horizontal line

A] 'V' Engine

B] Inline Engine

C] Opposed Engine

D] Radial Engine

274] Cylinders positioned in 'V' shape

A] 'V' Engine

B] Inline Engine

C] Opposed Engine

D] Radial Engine

275] Cylinders positioned radially

A] 'V' Engine

B] Inline Engine

C] Opposed Engine

D] Radial Engine

276] Cylinders arranged horizontally opposite to each other

A] 'V' Engine

B] Inline Engine

C] Opposed Engine

D] Radial Engine

293] What IS the reason for hissing noise from cylinder head?

A] excessive tappet clearance

B] wrong injection timing

C] pie-ignition

D] air cleaner mounting loose.

INDUSTRIAL TRAINING INSTITUTE

Monthly Test-11, Marks- 20, Date:- ________________

(Every Question Carry Two Marks)

294] Mounted on cylinder head or block

A] Fins

B] Radiators

C] Fan

D] Water pump

295] Allows fluid both way in and out of cylinder

A] Piston

B] Push Rod

C] Primary cup

D] Check valve

296] Relieves excess pressure of air from the air tank.

A] Air compressor

B] Unloader valve

C] Safety valve

D] Brake chamber

297] Regulates maximum air pressure, reaching to air tank.

A] Air compressor

B] Unloader valve

C] Safety valve

D] Brake chamber

298] Supplies air to front and rear brake

A] Brake actuator

B] Dual brake valve

C] System protection valve

D] Flick valve

299] Operated for parking the vehicle.

A] Brake actuator

B] Dual brake valve

C] System protection valve

D] Flick valve

300] Distributes air to various circuits
A] Brake actuator
B] Dual brake valve
C] System protection valve
301] Keeps valves in closed position
A] Push Rod
B] Tappet
C] Spring
D] Cam lobe
302] Allow fuel to flow in and out
A] Valves
B] Coil spring
C] Diaphragm
D] Rocker arm
303] Allows coolants into the expansion tank
A] Pressure relief valve
B] Engine fan belt
C] Radiator drain plug
D] Over flow pipe

INDUSTRIAL TRAINING INSTITUTE
Monthly Test-12, Marks- 20, Date:- _______________
(Every Question Carry Two Marks)

304] An overflow valve is used
A] to send back excess fuel from the fuel filler
B] to supply more fuel to the fuel filter
C] to supply clean fuel
D]to take the leaking fuel
305] Feed pumps are driven by
A] camshaft of engine
B] Camshaft of FIP
C] Timing Gears
D] Varies from engine to engine.
306] The oil pumps are generally driven by
A] camshaft
B] rocker shaft
C] crankshaft
D] damper pulley
307]Engine develops less power due to

A]defective ignition timing

B]excessive rich mixture

C]defective lubrication system

D]too tight cylinder head

308] Creates pressure on fluid

A] Brake pedal

B] Master cylinder piston

C] Wheel cylinder piston

D] Distribution block

309] Pushes master cylinder piston through linkages.

A] Brake pedal

B] Master cylinder piston

C] Wheel cylinder piston

D] Distribution block

310] Actuates the piston

A] Piston

B] Push Rod

C] Primary cup

D] Check valve

311] Develops pressure on fluid

A] Piston

B] Push Rod

C] Primary cup

D] Check valve

312] Displacement volume of piston

A] |.H.P.

B] Swept volume

C] Mechanical efficiency

D] Horse power

313] Starting point of piston's downward movement in the cylinder

A] T.D.C.

B] Cycle

C] B.D.C.

D] Ignition